MW01000051

HENRY FORD

for KIDS

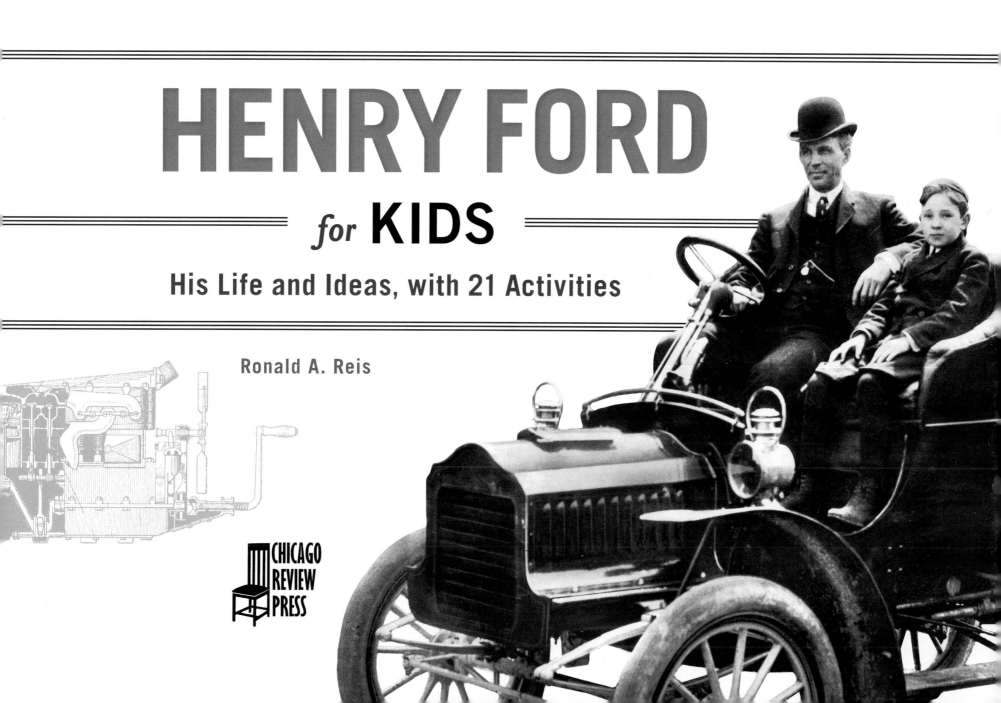

HENRY FORD

for KIDS

His Life and Ideas, with 21 Activities

Ronald A. Reis

CHICAGO
REVIEW
PRESS

Copyright © 2016 by Ronald A. Reis
All rights reserved
Published by Chicago Review Press Incorporated
814 North Franklin Street
Chicago, Illinois 60610
ISBN 978-1-61373-090-4

Library of Congress Cataloging-in-Publication Data
Are available from the Library of Congress.

Cover and interior design: Monica Baziuk
Cover images: Front cover (clockwise, from top left): Automobile traffic, Library of Congress LC-DIG-det-4a27910; Henry Ford (right) at the Edison Illuminating Company plant, From the Collections of The Henry Ford (P.188.606); Ford Motor Company, Library of Congress LC-DIG-det-4a27900; Women welding, Library of Congress LC-USZ62-111143; Henry and Edsel Ford in the Model F, © Corbis; four-cylinder Model T engine cutaway drawing, Wikimedia Commons. Back cover: Ford Motor Company Delivery Department, Library of Congress LC-USZ62-26766; Henry Ford and Barney Oldfield with the 999, From the Collections of The Henry Ford (P.188.4568).
Interior illustrations: James Spence

Printed in the United States of America
5 4 3 2 1

FOR MY GRANDSON THEO and his fourth-grade class at Wildwood Elementary School in Piedmont, California, with thanks for helping me test out some of the activities in this book. You are an awesome bunch.

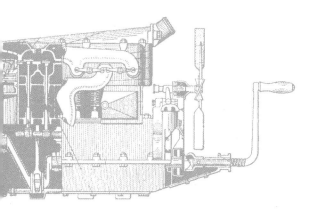

CONTENTS

NOTE TO READERS

There are two things it will be helpful for you to know as you read this book. First, the book contains a glossary, starting on page 110. All the glossary terms are in **bold** typeface upon their first appearance in the book.

Second, dollar amounts given in the book are contemporary figures. That means they are the amount for the time period discussed. You may want to convert some of the dollar figures to the equivalent amount today. One way to do this is to find an inflation calculator on the Internet, such as the US Inflation Calculator, www. usinflationcalculator.com. For example, in converting the $5-a-day figure Henry Ford paid many of his workers in 1914 to a 2015 dollar amount, you would arrive at $116.85. Regardless of the year in which you're reading this book, you can use an inflation calculator to convert monetary values from Henry Ford's time to today.

INTRODUCTION

Henry Ford did not invent the **automobile**. He was not the first to place an engine inside a buggy, thus creating a **horseless carriage**. What Henry Ford did do with the automobile, however, gave birth to a modern America.

Before Henry Ford, cars were owned mostly by the wealthy. "If there were no Fords," it was said, "automobiling would be like yachting—the sport of the rich." In 1900, just 4,192 automobiles were registered in the United States. With Henry Ford's introduction of the Model T in 1908, that number grew rapidly. By 1910, 181,000 cars traveled the streets and highways of America. By 1920, there were almost two million.

Henry Ford made such phenomenal growth happen. "I will build a motorcar for the multitude," he declared. "It will be large enough for the family but small enough for the individual to run and care for. It will be constructed of the best materials, by the best men to be hired, after the simplest designs that modern engineering can devise. But it will be so low in price that no man making a good salary will be unable to own one—and enjoy with his family the blessings of hours of pleasure in God's great open spaces."

This book is the story of the man who did just that, and, by so doing, put America on wheels.

TIME LINE

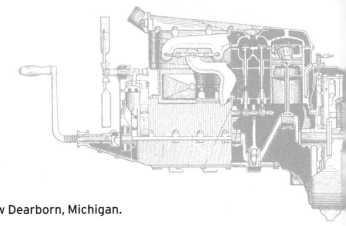

1863 Henry Ford is born on July 30 in what is now Dearborn, Michigan.

1879 Henry leaves home to work in Detroit as a machinist.

1882 Ford returns to Dearborn to operate steam-engined farm equipment.

1888 Henry Ford marries Clara Jane Bryant.

1892 Husband and wife move to Detroit, where Ford takes a job as an engineer at the Edison Illuminating Co.

1893 Henry and Clara's only child, Edsel, is born on November 6.

1896 Ford completes his Quadricycle.

Ford meets his idol, Thomas Edison, in New York City.

1899 The Detroit Automobile Company is formed; Ford becomes chief engineer. Venture fails.

1901 The Henry Ford Company is formed with Ford as engineer.

1903 The Ford Motor Company is founded.

First Model A is offered for sale.

1906 Henry Ford becomes president of the Ford Motor Company.

1908 Ford begins manufacturing the Model T.

1910 The Ford Motor Company begins operations at the Highland Park factory.

1913 First automobile moving assembly line is introduced at Highland Park.

1914 Henry Ford announces his plan for workers: $5.00 wage, eight-hour day, with profit sharing.

1915 Henry Ford's "Peace Ship," the *Oscar II*, sets sail for Norway on a mission to end World War I.

1916 ⚙ Edsel marries Eleanor Clay.

1917 ⚙ Construction of Rouge River factory begins.
Will take 10 years to complete.

1918 ⚙ Ford loses his bid for a US Senate seat.

1919 ⚙ Edsel Ford becomes president of the Ford Motor Company.

1920 ⚙ Publication of Ford's anti-Semitic views begins
in the *Dearborn Independent*.

1922 ⚙ The Ford Motor Company acquires Lincoln Motor Company.

1927 ⚙ Production of Model T ends. The new Model A is
produced at the Rouge River plant.

1929 ⚙ Light's Golden Jubilee celebrates the founding of Greenfield Village,
Henry Ford's large outdoor museum, on October 21.

⚙ Stock market crashes on October 29,
bringing on the Great Depression.

1932 ⚙ Ford Hunger March takes place on March 7; four people are shot dead.

⚙ Ford introduces a low-cost V-8 automobile.

1937 ⚙ Violent Battle of the Overpass, at which Ford
security forces attack union organizers.

1941 ⚙ Ford signs contract with United Auto Workers.

1943 ⚙ Edsel Ford dies at age 49.

⚙ Henry Ford again elected president of Ford Motor Company.

1945 ⚙ Henry resigns as president of Ford Motor Company.

⚙ Henry's grandson Henry Ford II becomes
president of Ford Motor Company.

1947 ⚙ Henry Ford dies at Fair Lane on April 7, at age 83.

Henry Ford's birthplace,
in rural (at the time)
Dearborn, Michigan.

From the Collections of the Henry Ford (P.O.995)

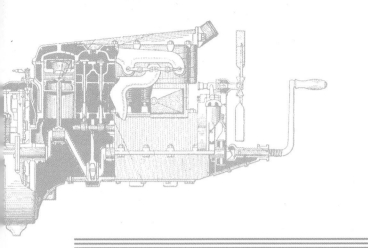

FARM BOY MECHANIC

Henry Ford was born to William and Mary Ford on July 30, 1863, in Dearborn, Michigan, a rural farm town eight miles west of Detroit. The oldest of six children, Henry claimed to the day he died that the monotony of farming was his inspiration for creating all things mechanical. "I have followed many a weary mile behind a plow and I know all the drudgery of it," Ford wrote. "What a waste... when in the same time a tractor could do six times as much work."

Henry's father, William, fled Ireland at the age of 21, during the great potato famine of 1847. William's parents, two brothers, and four sisters made the dangerous Atlantic voyage to the United States along with him. Though

William was called a boy in the Irish tradition (because his father was still alive), he was very much a man. Described as "of medium height, with a muscular strength, gray eyes, and a serious demeanor," William arrived in America already a skilled carpenter. He would put his talents to good use as a farmer.

Mary, Henry's mother, met William in Dearborn, where the Fords had settled. Though William was 14 years older than Mary, he was willing to wait until the brown-haired, dark-eyed girl graduated from high school before asking her to marry him. Their wedding took place in Detroit, on April 25, 1861.

The Fords had six children, four boys and two girls, yet none gave them the pride of their firstborn—Henry.

As a toddler, Henry took to the Fords' prosperous Dearborn farm as any curious child would. The land was fertile, with evergreen shrubs, an orchard, and well-cultivated fields of wheat, corn, and hay. Patches of timber were filled with wild creatures. Henry became familiar with the small native animals among the trees: skunks, raccoons, foxes, minks, muskrats, and rabbits. Henry Ford's earliest recollections were of the forest at the back of the farm.

"The first thing I remember in my life," Ford wrote decades later, "is my father taking my brother and myself to see a bird's nest under a big oak.... John was so young that he could not walk. Father carried him. I being two years older could run along with him.... I remember the nest with four eggs and also the bird and hearing it sing."

Memories such as this one gave young Henry a great love of nature that would last a lifetime. Those memories were mingled with his fondness and admiration for his father. Henry recalled his dad turning the plow aside to spare a bird's nest.

In his early years, Henry saw his father as a firm, caring man. He viewed his mother as his moral teacher. "You must earn the right to play," Mary

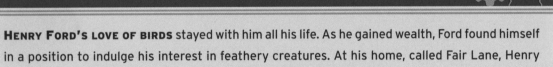

Ford "Bird Hotels"

HENRY FORD'S LOVE OF BIRDS stayed with him all his life. As he gained wealth, Ford found himself in a position to indulge his interest in feathery creatures. At his home, called Fair Lane, Henry Ford set up a sanctuary for birds unlike anything in North America. It became the envy of every ornithologist (one who studies birds) the world over.

With close to 1,500 acres devoted to providing a home to 200 bird species, Ford hired an entire ground crew to take care of them. The nature lover had 200 multistory "bird hotels" placed throughout his estate. One such "hotel" was said to have 500 "rooms." In addition to the "hotels," there were dozens of birdbaths. Feeding stations were everywhere.

Henry and Clara liked nothing better than to sit on their sunporch at the rear of their house and, with binoculars in hand, watch the birds.

Once, the ground crew put white netting over two cherry trees near the house. They wanted to protect the fruit for use in cooking and preserving. When Henry Ford went to work in the morning, he noticed a couple of robins entangled in the webbing. He tore the netting off. Later he scolded the men who had put it there, saying, "Don't put that back no matter who wants it back on there. There's plenty of cherries for the birds and us, too."

told her eldest son. "The best fun follows a duty done."

Such lectures had a strong impact on Henry. He carried them with him for the rest of his life. When people later asked Henry Ford what he remembered of his mother, he simply quoted her. "Life will give you many unpleasant tasks to do, and your duty will be hard and disagreeable and painful to you at times, but you must do it. You may have pity on others, but you must not pity yourself."

Henry Ford later said of his mother, giving her the highest compliment, "She was that rarest type, one who so loved her children that she did not care whether they loved her. What I mean by this is that she would do whatever she considered necessary for our welfare even if she thereby lost our good will."

TRAGEDY STRIKES

GROWING UP, Henry's relationship with his brothers and sisters was playful and teasing. However, as Henry grew older and began to tinker, the siblings got nervous. When toys arrived for birthdays and Christmas, someone would always shout: "Don't let Henry see them! He'll take them apart!" The brothers and sisters should not have worried. While many kids could disassemble such toys, Henry had also learned to put them back together. For Henry Ford, tools were his toys and always would be.

ACTIVITY
BUILD A BIRD FEEDER

HENRY FORD'S LOVE OF BIRDS led him to create a huge bird sanctuary, with dozens of bird feeders scattered about. In this activity, you build a simple bird feeder using a cup and saucer.

You'll Need
- Bird field guide or access to the Internet
- Cup (with handle) and saucer (preferably glass or ceramic)
- Epoxy glue (available at craft, hardware, or home supply stores)
- Set of acrylic paints and brush (optional)
- String (or twine), 10 to 12 feet (3 to 3.6 meters) long
- Birdseed
- Embellishments, such as stickers, beads, feathers, tiny trinkets, etc.

1. Find out what types of wild birds populate your area, so you will be able to identify the birds that use your feeder. Search the Internet or refer to a good field guide to local birds.

2. Glue your cup and saucer together, as shown. Be sure to place the cup in the center of the saucer, with the handle up. Follow instructions supplied with your glue. You may have to leave the glue to cure (finish drying) overnight.

3. Decorate your bird feeder. You might place bird stickers or glue on beads or feathers. Or you can paint flowers, birds, or various scenes of nature on the cup or saucer. If you are using paints, be sure to give the paint plenty of time to dry.

4. Tie a string (or piece of twine) around the handle of your bird feeder. Make sure the bird feeder hangs so that the saucer is parallel with the ground. If the string seems to slide up the handle, use a piece of tape to hold it where you want it.

5. Scatter birdseed in the cup, allowing it to spill out onto the saucer.

6. Hang your bird feeder from a tree branch that you can see easily. Choose a shady spot where you have seen birds spending time.

Be patient, it may take some time for birds to find your bird feeder and feel comfortable eating from it. There are about 800 species of birds in North America. You are sure to attract one or more.

At seven years of age (in 1871), Henry headed off to a one-room schoolhouse about two miles from his home. He proved to be a bright but unexceptional student.

It was in school that Henry developed his lifelong love of playing tricks on people. According to one account, "Henry once bored two small holes in the bottom of another student's seat. In one hole he hid a needle with the point up, and then ran a connecting string down through the other hole and under the bench to his seat. During a dead space in the school day, he yanked on the string, and the resulting howls brought loud laughter from his classmates."

On Henry's 13th birthday he was given a watch as a present. The teenager sat down, took the timepiece apart, and reassembled it. In no time Henry, the farm boy mechanic, learned to repair watches.

Fixing watches was for Henry the beginning of his love of mechanical devices. "Machines are to a mechanic what books are to a writer," he later said. "He gets ideas from them and if he has any brains he will apply them."

Though the Ford farm was doing well, bringing in a good yearly income, plenty of work was required to make that a reality. According to one of the Fords' neighbors, "Farmers set off for their fields and went to work from daylight to dark, and then went home and did their chores." All the Ford children were expected to do their share, too.

In the spring of 1876, the Fords prepared to welcome another member into the family. Mary Ford was pregnant again, and by all indications her eighth child would be delivered with little trouble. Her first infant had been stillborn (born dead) in 1861. But after that, Mary had a run of successful deliveries, with Henry (1863), John (1865), Marga-

A typical 19th-century midwestern farm. Henry Ford hated the drudgery of farming, spending long days behind a horse-drawn plow.

Library of Congress LC-DIG-fsa-8d35082 (photographer: Fenno Jacobs)

ret (1867), Jane (1869), William Junior (1871), and Robert (1873). As was the custom at the time, Mrs. Ford would be giving birth at home.

This time, unexplainably, something went terribly wrong. The baby was lost. Twelve days later, on March 29, Mary died. She was just 37 years old.

Henry Ford was emotionally devastated. His world was turned upside down. "I thought a great wrong had been done to me when my mother was taken," Henry later declared. "The house was like a watch without a mainspring."

DETROIT DREAMING

AT THE age of 17, Henry Ford had had enough of farm life. He was now through with school and restless to move on. Henry's experiences so far with things mechanical had whetted his appetite for more. Deep down inside, he felt he was meant to be a mechanic. To prove it, if to no one else but himself, young Henry would have to go to Detroit, to apprentice at a machine shop. At five feet eight inches tall, with a tough, wiry strength, Henry felt he was ready for the challenge.

On December 1, 1879, Henry Ford took off for Detroit, walking eight miles to the city. It took him half a day.

Henry didn't tell anyone he was leaving. His family discovered his absence only after Henry was gone. Though he never spoke of running away, the family knew he was about to make the move.

Some believe that William Ford was opposed to Henry going to Detroit. William, they said, felt Henry's future was in farming. Yet, according to Henry's sister Margaret, their father was OK with young Henry going. "My father was sympathetic and understanding of Henry's desire to supplement his mechanical training and education with actually working in a shop." Maybe William felt working in a hot, dirty machine shop would cure Henry of a desire to do so, and he would then head back home to a life on the farm.

The Detroit that Henry Ford arrived at in 1879 was still a small city. The 1880 census shows only 116,340 people. But there was a bustle to the place, with industrial activity everywhere, particularly along the Detroit River. Altogether, there were nearly 1,000 mechanical and manufacturing establishments. Upon arrival in the city, Henry rented a room and went out looking for a job.

Henry found immediate employment at the Michigan Car Company, which built streetcars. He was fired after just six days on the job, however. According to one account, "Henry quickly solved a problem in the construction process which a number of employees had worked all day trying to correct, thus embarrassing them and their foreman."

Henry had no trouble finding a second job, this one at the James Flower and Brothers Machine Shop, where he worked 60-hour weeks for a wage of $2.50 per week. To supplement his income, Henry took in watches and clocks to repair.

tion engine, it was Henry's introduction to what became his lifelong occupation—the making of gasoline-driven road vehicles.

"THE BELIEVER"

Though William Ford had gone along with Henry's desire to seek work as a machinist in Detroit, he never gave up trying to persuade his son to return to farming. After two years on his own, Henry gave in and went back to Dearborn in 1882. But the now 19-year-old son made it clear to his father he was not returning to be a farmer. Henry's days of milking cows and picking up a shovel were over.

Although Henry did move back into his father's house, the young man maintained his city interests. Henry Ford enrolled in night courses at Goldsmith, Bryant & Stratton Business College in Detroit, studying shorthand, typing, accounting, and drafting. He also worked part-time for the Westinghouse Engine Company as an expert in steam engines, traveling around the countryside fixing broken equipment for farmers and mill workers.

In 1886, William Ford offered his eldest son something too good to pass up. Henry's dad would give him 80 acres of prime farm- and forestland not far from where he lived. Henry took it, expanded the small house on the property, and went into business cutting and supplying lumber

Port Huron, near Detroit, at the time Henry Ford left the family farm for work as a machinist in the city.

Library of Congress LC-DIG-det-4a19478

After a few months at Flower Brothers, Henry moved on to the Detroit Dry Dock Engine Works, where he stayed two years. There, at the city's largest shipbuilding firm, Henry began working with motors. Most of the engines the young Ford labored on were powered by steam, but around this time Henry read about a curious engine that ran on gasoline. Known as an **internal combus-**

MAKE A LEMON-POWERED BATTERY

EARLY CAR MANUFACTURERS worked to develop a battery that could supply voltage, or energy, to operate an electrical starter motor. You can make a simple "battery" using lemons and two different metals.

You'll Need

- 4 white stickers or labels
- 4 big lemons
- Kitchen knife
- 4 pennies
- 4 iron nails
- Voltmeter (available from craft, hardware, electronics, or home supply stores)
- 5 alligator clips (available from craft, hardware, electronics, or home supply stores)
- Pencil and paper

Adult supervision required.

1. Using stickers, identify your lemons as A, B, C, and D.

2. Using the knife, cut a penny-sized slit in all four lemons. Insert a penny (your positive terminal) into each slit, but only halfway.

3. Push a nail (your negative terminal) into each lemon, placing it about 1 inch (2.5 centimeters) from the penny.

4. Using a voltmeter, measure and record the voltage for lemon A. To do this, attach the positive lead, or wire (usually red), to the penny, and the negative lead, or wire (usually black), to the nail. The measurement given on your voltmeter will be in millivolts (1 millivolt = 0.001 volts).

5. Repeat Step 4 for lemons B, C, and D. Determine the total voltage for all four lemons by adding together the voltage of each lemon. For example, if the lemons produce 316, 504, 140, and 180 millivolts, adding the individual voltages gives us 1,140 millivolts (or 1.140 volts).

6. Using alligator clips, connect the four lemons in a series. An alligator clip goes from the nail in lemon A to the penny in lemon B. Continue in the same way, connecting lemon B to lemon C, and lemon C to lemon D.

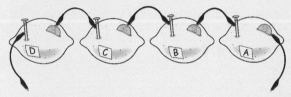

7. Connect one alligator clip to the penny in lemon A and another alligator clip to the nail in lemon D.

8. Measure and record the voltage across all four lemons by connecting the voltmeter leads to the hanging alligator clips. The total voltage for all four lemons should be close to the sum you arrived at in step 5.

While your lemon battery can actually produce a useful voltage, the resulting electricity produced is quite low. It is only about one milliampere (0.001 of an ampere). That would not be enough current to light even the tiniest lightbulb.

Henry Ford (far right with mustache) at the Edison Illuminating Company plant, around 1895, at the age of 32.

From the Collections of the Henry Ford (P.188.606)

to neighbors, shipyards, factories, and shops in Detroit. At least it was not farming.

All this work, with little play, had made Henry, now 22 years old, seem a dull man. To improve his social life, Henry took dancing lessons, learning the waltz and the polka.

On New Year's Eve, 1885, Henry Ford attended a dance at the Martindale House in nearby Greenfield. A tall, handsome man, who was also a good dancer, Ford had every confidence he would find a "mash" (sweetheart) for the evening.

There, he was introduced to a petite local girl of 18, named Clara Jane Bryant. After a few dances, Ford reached into his pocket and pulled out an unusual double-dialed watch he had made, one that told both railroad and "sun" time. Clara was enthralled. Returning home that evening, she told her mother, "He's different. He didn't just chatter about the music or talk about people. He's a serious-minded person."

Henry later told his sister Margaret that after 30 seconds of conversation with Clara Bryant, he knew she was the one for him.

The couple began courting, or dating, in the early winter of 1886. Henry owned a sleek, forest-green, low-slung sleigh called a **cutter**. They went to ice-skating parties. In the spring they took buggy rides and went on picnics. In keeping with the custom at the time, all their outings were strictly chaperoned.

On April 19, 1886, Clara and Henry became engaged. But it would be two more years before they got married. Henry had little money and needed to work hard and accumulate a respectable savings before the two could rightfully marry. Finally, on April 11, 1888 (Clara's birthday), they were married at her parents' house. The couple built a new home on Henry's property, and they moved in June 1889.

From the beginning of their marriage, Clara had great confidence in her husband and whatever he chose to do. When Henry began to talk of developing a gas-powered horseless carriage, Clara was enthusiastic and supportive. Henry soon started calling her "The Believer." Clara would always be there, believing in every move Henry Ford would make.

Clara Ford in 1888, the year she married Henry Ford, at the age of 22. From the Collections of the Henry Ford (P.O.867)

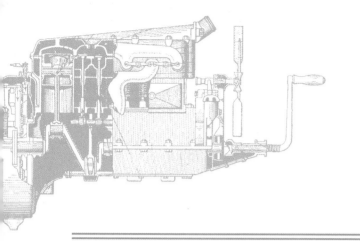

THE FORD MOTOR COMPANY

After their marriage, Clara and Henry seemed to be settling into life in the country. Yet, it was not to be. One day, after repairing a gas engine used for sawing lumber on the farm, Henry sat Clara down for a serious talk. Ford told his wife he was convinced that a gasoline engine could be adapted to a road-going vehicle. In September 1891, the Fords moved back to Detroit, where Henry took an engineering job at the Edison Illuminating Company. It was the perfect place for him to learn everything he could about electricity and mechanics.

In his spare time, Ford began experimenting with materials necessary to make his own internal combustion engine. It was also at this time, in late 1893, that Clara gave birth to a baby boy. The couple named him Edsel, after a close high school friend of Henry's. Edsel was Clara and Henry's only child.

The Bagley Avenue workshop in Detroit, Michigan, where Henry Ford built his first car, the Quadricycle.
From the Collections of the Henry Ford (P.188.9378)

By Christmas Eve 1893, the budding inventor was ready to demonstrate his "tabletop model" to Clara. Built of discarded metal parts, and looking like a toy cannon mounted on a board, Ford spun its **flywheel** while Clara trickled gasoline into its intake port.

Nothing happened at first. Then, according to historian Douglas Brinkley, "On the second attempt the crude little engine coughed to life and then into flames, filling the Ford kitchen with foul-smelling black smoke and making a terrible racket. The experiment was a triumph, though, even to Clara."

Behind his house in Detroit, Henry had a tiny shed with a workbench inside. It was here, in 1896, that Ford began (with the help of some friends from the Edison Company) to build his first automobile, known as the **Quadricycle**.

The Quadricycle had four bicycle wheels. Its power source, a twin-cylinder engine, produced four **horsepower** (enough to equal four horses pulling a wagon). The engine itself was air cooled, though Ford later added water jackets—a water-filled casing that helps control the engine's temperature.

Power was delivered to the car's rear **axle** through a drive chain and sprocket. The cart-like machine had no brakes. Steering was by a lever.

In the early morning of June 4, 1896, Ford and an assistant were ready to take the Quadricycle out for its first test drive. But, to both men's horror, they realized a terrible oversight. "In his determination to build the vehicle," reported biographer Stephen Watts, "Ford had failed to notice that it was too large to fit through the shed door. Ford grabbed an ax and doubled the opening by knocking out some bricks. The pair then wheeled the Quadricycle out onto the cobblestoned alley."

Henry Ford had done it. He had built his own **internal combustion engine** and mounted it in a vehicle. Ford had constructed a horseless carriage. He had an automobile.

THOMAS EDISON GIVES THE WORD

BY THE summer of 1896, Henry Ford had become a highly regarded Edison Illuminating Company chief engineer. As a reward for his service, the president of Edison, Alexander Dow, invited Ford to accompany him to the company's 17th annual convention in New York City.

Ford jumped at the chance to go. It provided the auto inventor the opportunity to at least see, if not actually meet, a legendary pioneer. The convention's guest of honor was Thomas Alva Edison, whom Ford had idolized since boyhood for turning night into day with his invention of the **incandescent** electric lightbulb.

Edison, known as the Wizard of Menlo Park (in New Jersey), secured more than 1,000 patents in his lifetime. Recognized for squeezing at

The Ford Quadricycle in 1896.
Wikimedia Commons

least twice as much work out of a day as any ordinary person, Edison was known to say, "Genius is one percent inspiration, ninety-nine percent perspiration."

At the convention's grand banquet, Ford was introduced to Edison as, "This young fellow who has made some sort of car he runs with gasoline."

Cupping an ear, because he was nearly deaf, Edison asked to hear more about it. Henry Ford came and sat beside Edison, took out a pencil, and began sketching on the back of a menu as he explained his Quadricycle in detail.

Suddenly, Edison took his hand from his ear and slapped Ford on the back.

"Young man, you have the right idea," Edison yelled. "Keep right at it. This car has the advantage over the electric car because it supplies its own power."

Ford later told his wife that what he heard from Edison that night was just the inspiration he needed. "Well, you won't be seeing much of me for the next year," Henry said to Clara.

Ford was now bursting with confidence. "No man up until that time had given me any encouragement," he recalled. "I had hoped I was right, sometimes I knew I was, sometimes I only wondered if I was, but here … out of a clear sky the greatest inventive genius in the world had given me a complete approval."

Ford immediately sold his Quadricycle for $200 (he later bought it back) and started work on a second car. But to make not only another car but many more after that, Ford needed money—lots of it. He needed investors who were willing to help him transform his invention into production automobiles.

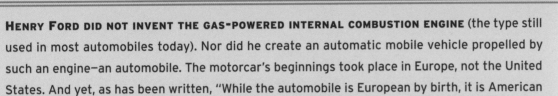

Europe Out in Front

HENRY FORD DID NOT INVENT THE GAS-POWERED INTERNAL COMBUSTION ENGINE (the type still used in most automobiles today). Nor did he create an automatic mobile vehicle propelled by such an engine—an automobile. The motorcar's beginnings took place in Europe, not the United States. And yet, as has been written, "While the automobile is European by birth, it is American by adoption."

Self-propelled vehicles for use on roads began with steam-driven machines. By the mid-1800s, the United Kingdom had developed steam-operated buses that had limited success.

Steam was not the way to go, however. Such a form of propulsion was too expensive and inefficient for supplying small amounts of power.

As far back as 1860, a Belgian mechanic named Etienne Lenoir developed a two-cycle internal combustion engine (the simpler type used in lawn mowers today). It was the first of its kind. And though it was crude, it did work.

In 1878, Nicholas August Otto, a German, produced a four-cycle engine. It, too, was a clumsy machine. Neither man made any attempt to attach his engine to a vehicle.

The credit for combining an internal combustion engine with a carriage goes to Karl Benz in Germany. In 1885, the inventor created what is considered to be the first horseless carriage, by building a gas-burning tricycle.

The design credit for the first true automobile **prototype** goes to a Frenchman named Emile Constant Levassor. In 1891, Levassor produced a car with a gas engine in the front. The engine's weight up front helped hold the vehicle to the road. The rest of the chassis (supporting frame) accommodated the passengers.

The automobile had arrived!

EARLY CAR COMPANY FAILURES

THIRTY-SEVEN-YEAR-OLD HENRY Ford was now ready to become a professional automobile maker. To head off such an occurrence, the Edison Company offered Ford a promotion, but only if he would give up working on gas engines. "I had to choose between my job and my automobile," Ford recalled. "I chose the automobile."

ACTIVITY
DEMONSTRATE GEAR ACTION

GEARS (TOOTHED WHEELS) are used in bicycles and automobiles. They work together to change the rotational direction of shafts or speed up or slow down motion.

You'll Need
- Corrugated (alternating ridges and groves) cardboard, approximately 12 inches by 18 inches (30.5 centimeters by 45.7 centimeters)
- Ruler
- Scissors
- Pencil
- Drawing compass
- Tweezers
- Glue
- Masking tape
- Permanent marker (black)
- 2 pushpins

1. Cut out a piece of cardboard 8 inches by 8 inches (20.3 centimeters by 20.3 centimeters) to use as a base.

2. Using another piece of cardboard, trace two circles with the compass: 1½ inches (3.8 centimeters) and 3 inches (7.6 centimeters) in diameter. Cut out the circles.

3. Using another piece of cardboard, cut a strip ¼-inch (0.64-centimeter) wide across the corrugates, the length of the circumference for the smaller circle. Do the same for the larger circle.

4. Use tweezers to carefully remove the thin paper on one side of the corrugated cardboard strip.

5. Spread glue around the edge of your small circle.

6. Roll the corrugated cardboard around the circle, making sure the bumps are on the outside. Secure the strip with a piece of tape until the glue dries.

7. Repeat for the large circle. Now you have two "gears."

8. Make a mark with a marker on one tooth of each gear. You do this to track when each gear has made a rotation.

9. Attach the gears to your base, using pushpins at the center of each, while making sure the gear teeth interlock.

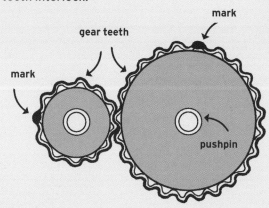

10. Rotate the larger gear clockwise. Which way does the smaller gear turn?

11. Using the marks to keep track, turn the large gear once. How many times does the small gear turn? Now, turn the small gear once. How many times does the large gear turn?

What are your conclusions about the direction of gear rotation and the number of turns one gear makes compared to the other?

Because gears transmit motion in predictable ways, they are useful in machines that require exact motion, from tiny watches to automobile **transmissions.**

Ford's first automotive business venture came with the Detroit Automobile Company, founded on August 5, 1899. On January 12, 1900, the company, of which Henry Ford was part owner and chief engineer, produced its first vehicle—a delivery wagon.

The Detroit Automobile Company hoped to produce a stream of horseless carriages that the public would line up to buy. As chief engineer, it was Ford's job to design and supervise the construction of a prototype (an original model) car. Once such a vehicle had been built, he was to get it into production as soon as possible.

The delivery wagon was the company's prototype. Unfortunately, it was not a particularly good automobile, and it had taken Ford an agonizingly long time to make. The company's chief engineer spent too much time dallying around, coming and going. "Henry never put much time in the shop," recalled Fredrick Strauss, a friend. "He might come in every day for an hour or two."

Henry Ford's problem with the prototype was typical of many engineers then as now. They do not know when to freeze their design. Engineers are forever wanting to change things; to improve them. To an engineer, the design job is never done.

For manufacturing people, however, there comes a time when enough is enough. They want to put the prototype into production.

After spending $86,000 trying to develop a car that could be made in quantity, the patience of the company's board of directors ran out. The Detroit Automobile Company was dissolved in January 1901 after nearly a year and a half in operation.

RACECAR CELEBRITY

UNKNOWN TO investors, some of the $86,000 the Detroit Automobile Company had spent had gone to develop a racecar. Ford had become convinced that the public's confidence in early automobile technology was based on speed. The faster a car could go, the better it was, and so, too, the company that produced it. Henry Ford was determined to enter the mushrooming racecar circuit.

With the help of ace mechanic Ed "Spider" Huff and design engineer C. Harold Wills, Ford worked night and day, in the dead of winter, to complete the racer. According to Alfred P. Sloan Jr., who would go on to lead General Motors, "When the shop where Ford and Wills worked got too cold for them to grip their pencils, they donned boxing gloves, and whaled away at each other until their blood flowed fast enough to warm them up, upon which the two men quietly returned to analyzing the **schematics** on their drawing boards."

The racecar that was finally produced generated 26 horsepower, weighed 2,200 pounds, and had 36-inch wire wheels. Steering was on the right side.

Ford's opportunity to race came on October 10, 1901. A one-mile dirt horse-racing track called the

Grosse Pointe Racetrack, located outside of Detroit, was the site. Though five participants were scheduled for the big competition, by race time three had withdrawn. The contest, with its $1,000 prize money, came down to Ford against a high-spirited Scotsman from Cleveland named Alexander Winton.

When the starting gun sounded, the mob of 7,000 onlookers rose to clap. Ford drove his car, while Huff kneeled on the auto's **running boards** to provide balance. Winton, alone, was behind the wheel of his 40-horsepower "Bullet" racer.

Winton took an early lead. For the first five laps, Ford trailed, as Winton's tires sprayed him and Huff with mud. But once Ford got the hang of driving, particularly on the turns, he began to pull up. On the seventh lap, Winton's engine started smoking. He fell hopelessly behind.

Ford and Huff were the only ones to cross the finish line, completing the 10 miles in 13 minutes and 23.8 seconds. Ford's car averaged an impressive speed—nearly 45 miles per hour. "Boy, I'll never do that again," Henry Ford announced as he picked up his prize money. "I was scared to death."

THE 999—FAST AND FURIOUS

FORD'S GROSSE Pointe victory attracted the attention of investors who were ready to back him in a new venture, to the tune of $30,000. On November 30, 1901, the Henry Ford Company came into existence, with Ford once more taking the title of engineer.

This second company ended as the first, and for more or less the same reasons. Ford had the racing bug, and he wanted to concentrate on a new, more powerful racing car. He was not yet ready to mass-produce cars for sale to the public. Ford resigned from the company that bore his name in March 1902.

Henry Ford and Spider Huff driving their 1901 racecar against Alexander Winton in the Grosse Pointe competition. From the Collections of the Henry Ford (P.288.10038)

CONSTRUCT A SIMPLE ELECTRIC MOTOR

AN ELECTRICAL MOTOR CHANGES electrical energy into mechanical motion. It is one of the most important inventions of all time. Almost from the beginning, Ford and other car makers sought to use electrical motors in their vehicles. These motors did not power the automobile. They operated various accessories (extras). Today, a typical car has dozens of electrical motors.

You are going to make the simplest motor possible.

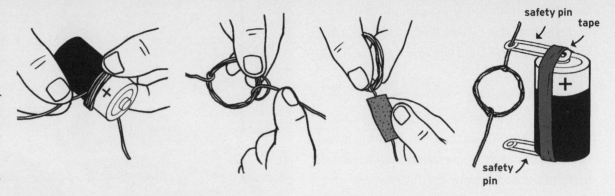

safety pin
tape
safety pin

You'll Need

- ⚙ Length of 24-gauge enamel-covered copper wire, approximately 36 inches (0.9 meters) long
- ⚙ 1½-volt D-size battery
- ⚙ Strip of general purpose sandpaper
- ⚙ 12-inch (30.5-centimeter) strip of masking tape
- ⚙ 2, 2-inch (5-centimeter) safety pins
- ⚙ 2 magnets, the type used on refrigerator doors

1. Wind the wire coil tightly around the battery 10 to 12 times, leaving 2 inches of wire stretched outward on both ends.

2. Carefully slip the wire coil off the battery, and tie each coil end with a few turns.

3. Using sandpaper, scrape the enamel (insulation) from the coil ends, *but only from half the diameter of the copper wire*. The exposed copper must be on the same side for each end of the wire.

4. Using tape, fix the two safety pins to the battery cell, and insert the coil ends into the "eyes" of the safety pins.

5. Hold the battery cell in one hand, and with the other hand, hold a magnet. Give your coil a spin and quickly bring the magnet close to (but not touching) the coil. Your coil should keep spinning. If your coil refuses to spin on its own, try two magnets for greater strength.

If you leave your motor unused for a few days, the bare wire may become oxidized. You should scrape the wire clean again before spinning your motor.

Also, do *not* leave the coil in place (between the safety pins) when the motor is not being used. The battery will overheat.

Your motor, which has converted electrical energy into mechanical motion, may not be very powerful, but it does spin.

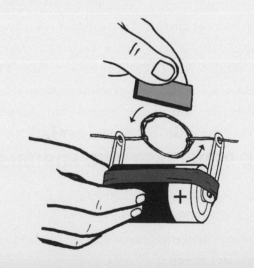

Ford's new racecar, known as the 999, was a true monster of the racetrack. Measuring nine feet by five feet, the 999 had four cylinders that were as big around as logs. The car, built by Ford and a fresh team of mechanics, had no windshield. It used a **tiller** instead of a steering wheel. Flames spurted out from its four exhausts. The 999 was rated at 70 horsepower.

Driving, or rather riding, the 999 was an experience all its own. "I cannot quite describe the sensation," Ford told a newspaper reporter. "Going over Niagara Falls would have been but a pastime after a ride in the 999."

Clara Ford absolutely forbade Henry from driving the new car in any race. For that, Ford hired a daredevil bicyclist named Barney Oldfield. Brash and dashing, the 24-year-old "No Fear" Oldfield had never driven a car in his entire life. But he was up for the challenge. Indeed, he would go on to drive in more than 2,000 car races before dying a peaceful death in 1946, 28 years after retiring from the sport.

The 999's first race, with Oldfield wearing what became his trademark goggles, took place on October 25, 1902, in Grosse Pointe Township. Known as the Manufacturers' Challenge Cup, it pitted Ford's car against none other than the one driven by Alexander Winton.

Fears for Oldfield's safety were real. Given his lack of experience, he was urged by many to drop out and let someone else drive. "Well, this chariot

may kill me," Oldfield responded, "but they will say afterward that I was going like hell when she took me over the bank."

The 999 won the five-mile contest by a full lap, breaking the US record time of 5 minutes, 28 seconds. A few weeks later, the car set a world record for the mile in one minute, one second.

Once again, winning a race put Ford back in business. His success attracted yet another group

Henry Ford and Barney Oldfield with the five-feet-by-nine-feet, four-cylinder, 70-horsepower 999 racecar. From the Collections of the Henry Ford (P.188.4568)

of investors willing to bet that a third time was the charm. They believed that Henry Ford was finally ready to settle down and do what he said he always intended to do—build a production car for the masses.

The first factory of the Ford Motor Company (1903–1904), known as the Mack Avenue plant.

Library of Congress LC-DIG-det-4a27900

THE FORD MOTOR COMPANY

ON JUNE 16, 1903, the Ford Motor Company was organized. With changes and growth, it is the company that still exists today.

Ford Motor started with $28,000 in the bank. That amount soon dropped by half. By early July there was only $223 on hand.

Not a single car had yet been sold. **Creditors** were beginning to think that Henry Ford was about to drop the ball again and strike out for the third time.

But they were wrong. On July 15, a Chicago dentist named Edward Pfennig became the first Ford retail customer. His check for $850 was quickly deposited in the Ford Motor Company bank account.

The car Dr. Pfennig purchased was a Model A (not to be confused with the later Model A produced in 1927). The car was put together at the company's assembly plant on Mack Avenue in Detroit. The factory had been an old wagon shop, and after 12 weeks of remodeling, a workforce of a dozen men, earning $1.50 a day, moved in on April 1.

At this time, the Ford Motor Company was strictly an assembly operation. No car parts were actually manufactured by Ford. Engines, transmissions, and axles, for example, came from the Dodge Brothers Machine Shop. The new company obtained its wooden bodies and cushions from the C. R. Wilson Carriage Company. The Prudden Company built the Model A's wheels. And the Hartford Rubber Works Company provided tires.

The Model A automobile was an example of Ford's "keep it simple and light" design philosophy. It was limited to a mere eight horsepower, produced by a twin-cylinder engine of Ford's own design. Maximum speed for the Model A was 25 miles per hour. It basically had no brakes. Yet, even with its limitations, the Model A was a success.

The Ford Motor Company went on to produce and sell a number of different model cars in the years immediately after its founding.

There was even a third, significant race to be noted. On January 1, 1904, a bitterly cold winter day, a modified Model B was brought out to frozen Lake St. Clair northeast of Detroit. Though Henry Ford swore he would never drive a racecar again, he did so on this day. The car crossed a measured mile in 39.25 seconds—91.3 miles per hour. "That put Model B on the map," Ford announced.

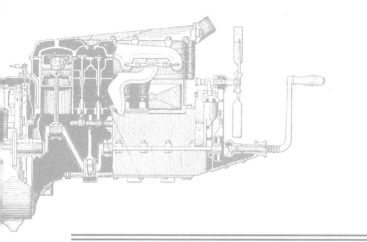

3

TIN LIZZIE

The Ford Motor Company was a roaring success from the beginning. Though Oldsmobile (known at the time as the Olds Motor Works), the industry leader, produced 5,000 to 6,000 cars in the 1903-4 period, Ford delivered 1,700 during the same time. Not bad! By mid-1905, Ford was turning out 25 cars a day. Sales for the year reached $1.91 million. The Ford Motor Company now employed 300 people, twice as many as the year before. The Mack Avenue factory was bursting at the seams.

In response, a larger manufacturing facility, known as the Piquette Avenue plant, opened in late 1905. It was ten times the size of the Mac Avenue factory.

Additionally, the three-story building was designed as an assembly plant from the ground up.

In the beginning, the Piquette Avenue factory produced a number of Ford models, some successful, a few of them not. But in 1906, when the company introduced the Model N, Henry Ford knew he had a winner. Priced at $500 and weighing only 1,000 pounds, the car could reach 40 miles per hour. Almost 9,000 Model N automobiles were sold in that breakout year.

Soon after, Models R and S hit the streets, and both were successes. Together, the N, R, and S

A Model T Ford (Tin Lizzie) in 1908, the car that put Americans on wheels. Library of Congress LC-USZ62-21222

proved a fundamental principle on which Ford was about to stake the company's future. The public, Henry Ford believed, was ready for a mass-produced, low-priced car, one that both farmers and city dwellers could afford.

During the winter of 1906–7, Ford directed that a private, locked work area be created on the third floor of the Piquette Avenue factory. Access was strictly limited to Henry Ford and a group of highly talented company designers and engineers.

The automobile to eventually emerge from this hidden research laboratory, the Model T, became the most famous car ever made. By 1927, its last year in production, more than 15 million had been sold. Designed and priced for the great multitude, the Model T was to change forever how Americans worked, played, and lived. It gave birth to a modern America.

In the secured room, designs were roughed out in chalk on four large blackboards. The chalk renderings were then turned into working drawings (**blueprints**) by highly specialized drafters. Working from the blueprints, skilled artisans made **patterns**, **molds**, and **mock-ups**. The Model T consisted of more than 5,000 individual parts (including tiny screws and nuts).

A key to the Model T's success as a lightweight and sturdy automobile was its use of **vanadium steel** in more than half its components. The story of this amazing metal's discovery by the Ford

Motor Company is in dispute, but according to Henry Ford:

In 1905, I [Henry Ford] was at a motor race at Palm Beach. There was a big smash-up and a French car was wrecked.... I thought the foreign cars had smaller and better parts than we knew anything about. After the wreck I picked up a little valve strip stem. It was very light and very strong. I asked what it was made of. Nobody knew. I gave the stem to my assistant. "Find out all about this," I told him. "That is the kind of material we ought to have in our cars."

The Model T was introduced to the world in October 1908. While Henry Ford had considerable help in creating the automobile, he deserves the most credit for "the car that put the world on wheels."

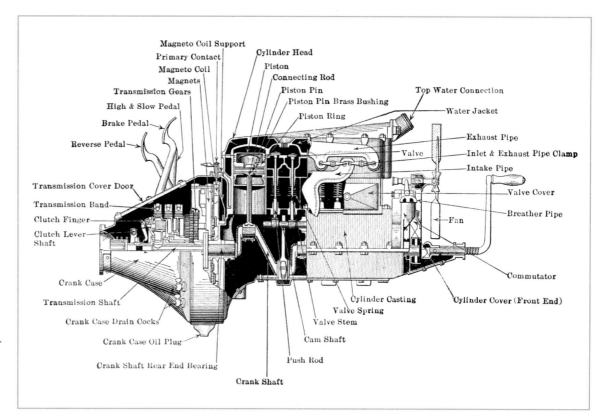

OCEAN TO OCEAN BY MODEL T

NINE MONTHS after Model Ts began pouring out of the Piquette Avenue factory, Ford, always mindful of publicity, saw another chance to gain it. A car race from New York City to Seattle, sponsored by the Alaska-Yukon-Pacific Exposition and the Automobile Club of America, was scheduled for June 1, 1909, and would be open to all comers. The distance, much of it on practically nonexistent roads, was 4,100 miles.

Though dozens of cars were scheduled to take part, only five actually raced. Two were Model T Fords. The Fords were stripped-down cars, weighing 950 pounds. Of the other entries, an Acme weighed 3,500 pounds; the Itala, 4,000 pounds; and the Shawmut, 4,500 pounds. It would be an endurance race between the light and the heavy, with Ford betting that light meant speed.

The rules of the road were strict. Each car engine was stamped—that is, marked with an identifying number and symbol so that the engine could not

A cutaway of the four-cylinder Model T Ford car engine, with its hand-crank starter. Wikimedia Commons

LEARN THE LANGUAGE OF INDUSTRIAL DRAWING

THE "LANGUAGE OF DRAWING" used in industrial production is called **orthographic projection**. An orthographic projection is a two-dimensional (2-D) picture of a three-dimensional (3-D) object. Anyone who makes or assembles anything needs to know how to read orthographic projection drawings. In this activity you will learn how!

You'll Need
⚙ Photocopier
⚙ Copy paper
⚙ 3 colored pencils: yellow, red, and blue

1. Study figures 1 and 2. There are six ways to view an object (figure 1). When making an orthographic

drawing, however, only three views are usually shown: front, top, and right side (figure 2).

2. Study the 3-D view in figure 3. Can you determine which orthographic projection represents the front view? What about the top and right

views? Note: the dotted lines indicate hidden surfaces.

3. Photocopy and enlarge figure 4. Use a yellow colored pencil to shade in the surfaces seen in the top view. Use a red colored pencil to shade in the surfaces for the front view. Finally, use a blue colored pencil to shade in the surfaces for the right side view.

FIGURE 3

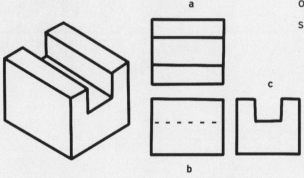

FIGURE 4

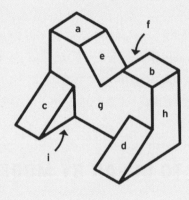

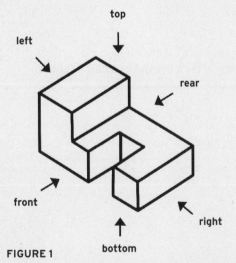

FIGURE 1

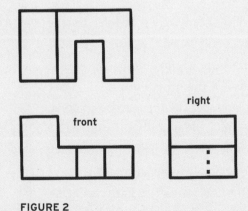

FIGURE 2

ANSWERS
Figure 3: front =B, top=A, right=C
Figure 4: Top View: surfaces A, E, F, B, C, D. Front View: surfaces G, C, D. Right Side View: surfaces H, I.

be swapped out for a new one along the way. Participants could obtain new parts at only two places, Chicago and Cheyenne. No car was allowed to travel on railway tracks. And there would be 30 checkpoints along the way.

While both Model T Fords crossed the Mississippi River at St. Louis two hours ahead of their nearest rival, they then hit a week of rain. "For seven days," wrote C. J. Smith, who drove the leading Ford, "we wore hip boots and rubber coats while the cars labored through Kansas gumbo [sticky soil] and Colorado and Wyoming mud and sand." There would be worse to come.

On June 22, the leading Ford struggled down the rugged Snoqualmie Pass, 90 miles east of Seattle. Even at that time of year, the gap was filled with five feet of snow in places. The route through the divide itself was little more than a wagon road.

A day later, on June 23, a Model T was the first to cross the finish line, completing the race in 23 days. The second Ford, having experienced major mechanical trouble, crossed the line 17 hours later.

"Mr. Ford's theory that a lightweight car, highly powered for its weight, can go places where heavier cars cannot go, and can beat heavier cars, costing five and six times as much, on the steep hills or bad roads, has been proved," announced Robert Guggenheim, the competition's organizer. "I believe Mr. Ford has the solution of the popular automobile."

But there was a catch! The judges discovered that Smith and Scott, drivers of the winning Ford, had violated race rules. The team evidently changed the engine for a portion of the run. Six months after the race, the Shawmut car became the official victor.

No matter. Ford Company executives had already distributed thousands of pamphlets, entitled, "The Story of the Race," to their dealers. And newspapers everywhere were quick to declare Ford the champion, with headlines such as FORD—WINNER OF THE OCEAN TO OCEAN CONTEST.

Two Model T Ford cars during the Transcontinental Race of 1909. From the Collections of the Henry Ford (P.188.72501)

HIGHLAND PARK AND THE MOVING ASSEMBLY LINE

In 1906, two years before the Model T's unveiling, Henry Ford bought 60 acres of land in Highland Park, on the northern end of Detroit. Ford was already thinking ahead. If demand for the Model T was anything like he was sure it would be, the Ford Motor Company would need a huge new factory where cars could be turned out by the hundreds daily.

The plant was designed by Albert Kahn, the leading industrial architect of the time. In its construction, the factory used poured concrete reinforced with steel rods. As a result, there were fewer interior columns. The main building was four stories high, 865 feet long, and 75 feet wide. Seventy-five percent of the wall space was glass—50,000 square feet of it.

The main reason Ford wanted lots of glass was so there would be plenty of light in the building. With more light, workers could see better. As a result, machines could be put closer together. More machines in less space meant higher productivity for a given floor space. Furthermore, with more open windows, there was better ventilation for the workers. Their health and well-being would improve.

The structure that opened on New Year's Day of 1910 was dubbed the Crystal Palace for all the light it let in.

But in order to build cars more rapidly and thus more profitably, it was not enough to construct a larger factory. If all one did was assemble automobiles in the same way as before, productivity would not increase. Ford and his associates had to develop a creative, revolutionary way of making Model Ts.

No one is quite sure where the inspiration for the continuously moving assembly line came from. Interestingly, it may have resulted from looking closely at the disassembly lines (assembly

In a publicity stunt, a Model T Ford climbs the steps of the YMCA building in Columbus, Nebraska, in 1911. From the Collections of the Henry Ford (P.O.2618)

MAKE A MOVING ASSEMBLY LINE

HENRY FORD IS CREDITED with developing the moving assembly line, where material to be assembled came to the workers, rather than the workers going to the material. In this activity, you set up a moving assembly line with 10 "workers."

You'll Need

⚙ You and 6 friends or classmates

⚙ Several copies of the car pieces on this page

⚙ Scissors

⚙ Glue

⚙ White paper

⚙ Colored pencils, crayons, or markers

⚙ Timepiece with second hand (Note: all smartphones have a stopwatch function)

1. Seven people are needed to assemble the Model A Ford. Preferably, individuals should be seated behind a row of tables, as on an assembly line.

2. Individuals are assigned various parts as follows:

> first person–*body*
> second person–*door with window*
> third person–*front fender*
> fourth person–*rear fender*
> fifth person–*front wheel*
> sixth person–*rear wheel*
> seventh person–*colors the car*

3. The first person cuts out the car *body*, glues it to a sheet of paper, and passes the auto to the second person. The second person cuts out the *door with window*, glues it in place, and passes the auto to the third person, and so on down the line to the seventh worker, who colors the car and then sets it aside for "shipment."

4. Someone with the timepiece should record the time it takes to complete each step, plus the total time. Then, with a second, third, and fourth go-round, record the times again. Does assembly time increase with practice?

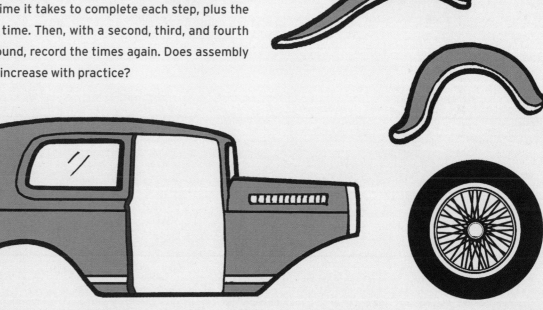

The magneto assembly line at the Highland Park plant that introduced the moving assembly line concept, 1913–14. From the Collections of the Henry Ford (P.833.167)

lines in reverse) used in the meatpacking industry. At Swift & Company, in Chicago, pigs were suspended upside down by one heel and moved that way from station to station.

According to Henry Ford, "The first step forward in assembly came when we began taking the work to the men instead of the men to the work. We believe a man shall never have to take more than one step, if possible, and that no man need ever stoop over."

In the process of breaking down a job, where a given worker does a small piece of the assembly, almost all independent thought was taken from the individual. "He does as nearly as possible only one thing with only one movement," Ford wrote. "The man who puts on the bolt does not put on the nut; the man who puts on the nut does not tighten it."

This type of assembly was first tried in April 1913, in putting together a **flywheel magneto**, an electrical generator that produces pulses of current. Used in the car's ignition system, the magneto provided power for the engine's spark plugs.

One workman doing a complete job had taken 20 minutes to assemble a unit. When what he did alone was spread over 29 operations, the assembly time was reduced to 13 minutes, 10 seconds. A year later, constructing the flywheel magneto was taking only 7 minutes. With more experimentation, the time dropped to just 5 minutes. According to Ford, "One man is now able to do

Auto Polo

AUTO POLO, WHICH BEGAN ITS RISE IN POPULARITY AROUND 1911, was often thought of as a bizarre sport. The motor sport was similar to equestrian polo, but automobiles (usually stripped-down Ford Model Ts) were used instead of horses.

Typically, two cars with two men each, a seat-belted driver and a mallet man, would compete against an opposing team of the same configuration. The object was to hit a regulation-sized basketball into a 15-foot-wide goal. While auto polo was sometimes played indoors, particularly in bad weather, most often competitions took place on an outdoor field, 300 feet by 120 feet. The cars would frequently hit top speeds of 40 miles per hour.

The first such auto polo match took place on July 20, 1911, in an alfalfa field in Wichita, Kansas. One team was known as the Red Devils, the other, the Gray Ghosts. All four competing cars were Model Ts. Close to 5,000 people witnessed the fun.

Safety was a big concern, both for participants and spectators. Cars often became entangled, with mallet men frequently thrown from the vehicles. The cars themselves rarely lasted for more than one event—if that. A single year—1924, when American and British teams competed—resulted in 1,564 broken wheels, 538 burst tires, 66 broken axles, 10 cracked engines, and 6 cars completely destroyed.

The sport lost its appeal in the late 1920s due primarily to the high cost of vehicle replacement.

Auto polo, a bizarre game using stripped-down Model T Ford cars. Library of Congress LC-DIG-ggbain-11114

somewhat more than four did only a comparatively few years ago."

These first Ford assembly lines, where the work moved but the workers did not, quickly spread to all operations. The key was in breaking down the job into small, individual operations. Previously, one person put together an entire motor. By 1914, the motor assembly was divided into 84 operations. The workers doing the work now did so three times faster than before.

THE $5-A-DAY REVOLUTION

THE ANNOUNCEMENT on January 5, 1914, amazed not only the automobile industry but the entire nation. Henry Ford, talking to reporters in his Highland Park auto plant, declared that starting on January 12, the Ford Motor Company would pay a minimum wage of $5 a day. Such a salary was twice the going rate in the automotive world.

There were many restrictions as to who actually qualified for the higher wage. Women, for example, were not included until 1916. Even then, they had to be single. Still, Ford's $5-a-day announcement drew hopeful employees from all over the world. Desperate to achieve the American dream of a stable, middle-class life, thousands of people mobbed the Ford Motor Company employment office.

The $5-a-day deal brought the Ford wage up from an average of $2.34 a day. The agreement also reduced the workday from nine to eight hours. As a result, the Ford Motor Company could now run three eight-hour shifts, Monday through Saturday. To staff the third shift, the company put out a call for 4,000 to 5,000 additional workers.

Would-be workers showed up in droves. As a result, Model Ts rolled off the assembly line in record numbers. Production was soon up to 793 cars a day, or 88 vehicles an hour—more than one automobile a minute.

But all was not well at Highland Park. Its 13,000 Ford workers were not happy. "Employees saw themselves as robot laborers; those with skills found that they were of little use on the assembly line with its endlessly repetitious activities," wrote the authors of *The Fords*. "Anyone who out produced another worker had to wait for him to catch up; the only virtue was dull efficiency."

All workers were victims of the **speedup**, a new term identified with the continuous moving assembly line. On the line, the belt would move a bit faster, so the worker would have to as well. "The chain system you have is a *slave driver*," wrote the wife of one worker to Henry Ford. "*My God!* Mr. Ford. My husband has come home and thrown himself down and won't eat his supper—so done out!"

This dissatisfaction resulted in a massive labor turnover rate. "So great was the alienation that in 1913 the Ford Motor Company had to hire 963 workers for every 100 it wanted to remain

A crowd of eager job applicants outside Highland Park plant after announcement of the Five Dollar Day by Henry Ford.

From the Collections of the Henry Ford (P.833.29)

33

CALCULATE TURNOVER RATE

TURNOVER IS WHEN EMPLOYEES leave a company and have to be replaced. A high turnover rate (percentage), whether voluntary or involuntary, is never a good thing, because it costs a company money to hire and train new employees. Both employers and employees suffer. The same sort of thing happens in your own life. If you are a participant in a school drama production with 46 students, but 12 have to be replaced, then the production is experiencing a turnover rate that could jeopardize the play.

In this activity, you are asked to calculate the employee turnover rate for three given situations. In all cases, the formula for finding the turnover rate (percentage) is:

(number of employees leaving ÷ the total employees) × 100 = turnover percentage

For example, if a company had 227 employees at the beginning of the year but had to replace 28 of them, the turnover rate is 12.3% ([28 ÷ 227] × 100 = 12.3%).

You'll Need
⚙ Notebook paper
⚙ Calculator
⚙ Pencil

1. If a company employed 100 people for a year, but six quit and nine were fired, what was the company's turnover rate?

2. If your school employed 15 teachers for a year, but for some reason all 15 had to be replaced at years' end, what was the staff turnover rate?

3. A school club had 18 members, but all were replaced. Six new members came on, but they all quit and had to be replaced. What was the club's turnover rate?

4. List three or four reasons why a high turnover rate would not be good for a company or group.

When the Ford Motor Company began to pay many of its workers $5 a day in 1914, its turnover rate dropped considerably. In 1915, it had to hire only 6,508 workers to keep its workforce at 52,000. Its turnover rate had fallen to just 12.5%.

ANSWERS FOR PROBLEMS 1–3:
(1) 15%; (2) 100%; (3) 133%

permanently on the payroll," noted one observer. "Accountants pointed out that it took $100 to train each one, and that the company was thus losing $3 million a year solely because of worker defections."

It was mainly because of this massive turnover of employees that Henry Ford and his chief executives decided, in 1914, to double the pay of the company's workers. There were a number of reasons for implementing the $5-a-day pay scale. There seemed to be a genuine interest in seeing workers share in company profits by being paid more. As a bonus, the executives hoped that many employees would then be able to buy the very product they were producing—Model Ts. But the key was still turnover rate—the company had to reduce it. Paying workers twice the going wage was Ford's answer.

And it worked!

In one story, the company's production chief, Bill Knudsen, asked a worker how he managed a huge jump in output. "Mr. Ford pay me two-fifty, he get 250 pieces," the Hungarian worker responded in broken English. "Mr. Ford now pay me five dollars a day, he get 500 pieces. I pay him back."

While the above conversation took place, with the employee talking to his boss, the laborer never lifted his eyes from his work, and kept on turning out parts.

In 1913, the Ford Motor Company personnel office had made 53,000 replacement hirings. In 1915, only 2,000 were required. Turnover at Ford was no longer a problem.

AMERICANIZING THE WORK FORCE

To QUALIFY for the $5-a-day wage, a male employee had to agree to take good care of his family. He had to live a moral, thrifty life, one free of drinking, smoking, and gambling. Women were not eligible for the higher wage unless they were single and supporting a family. Furthermore, if a man's wife worked outside of the home, he was not eligible to receive $5 a day in pay.

To guarantee such behavior, the Ford Motor Company set up a sociological department. At its peak, 150 investigators from the department were instructed to go out to homes and determine the living conditions of workers hoping to qualify for the $5-a-day payment.

In 1914, 71 percent of the company's employees were foreign born. At one point, 58 nationalities were represented, speaking more than 70 languages and dialects.

Half of those at Ford did not understand enough English to take instruction on the job. As a result, many immigrants were ordered to attend sociological department English classes established at the plant—before or after their shifts. Ford company staff taught the classes on a voluntary basis.

At the conclusion of an English course, participants went through an Americanization ceremony.

"Workers in the garb of their native countries descended from a stage into a symbolic 'melting pot,'" wrote Vincent Curcio. "From this pot they emerged dressed as Americans in stiff collars, ties, and suit jackets to receive a certificate confirming their newfound status as English speakers. As they did this they carried little American flags and sang 'The Star Spangled Banner.'"

A "melting pot ceremony" at the Ford English School, where workers entered wearing clothes from their country of origin and emerged in an American-style dress shirt, tie, and suit. From the Collections of the Henry Ford (P.O.7227)

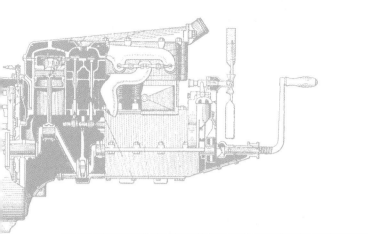

4

PEACE, WAR, AND POLITICS

By mid-1916, the Ford Motor Company had become so successful it reported a profit of $57 million. In addition, it had a cash-on-hand surplus of $52 million. The company owed not a dime to any bank or other institution.

What to do with such profits, with so much money? There are basically four ways a company can deal with this situation.

One, it can pay **stockholders** (owners of the company) large **dividends** (portions of the company's profits). When the Ford Motor Company was created in 1903, there were 12 stockholders, one of whom was Henry Ford. Receiving dividends, often on a yearly basis, had, by 1916, made these stockholders rich.

Two, the company can share its profits with employees in the form of higher wages. Ford did this when he increased the pay of his workers to $5 a day.

Three, a company can transfer profits to customers by way of lower prices. In 1908, a Model T **touring car** sold for $850. In 1916, the price had dropped to $360.

And four, the company can invest profits in improvements and expansion. Ford did that by building the Highland Park factory.

Henry Ford felt that while stockholders deserved a reasonable return on investment in the form of dividends, more was not justified. In fact, Ford went so far as to call stockholders who reaped big rewards for a meager investment, **parasites**.

In 1916, Henry Ford announced that he intended to earmark the bulk of the Ford Motor Company's $57 million in earnings for a new, massive expansion program. Future dividends, Ford declared, would just be tokens.

Two stockholders in particular, the Dodge brothers (John and Horace), were not pleased. The brothers had expansion ideas of their own. Having formed Dodge Brothers Motor Cars to make their own automobiles, they wanted to take production to a higher level. To do that, they would need to receive regular, high-paying dividends. Seeing that Ford intended to deny them the dividends they felt they earned, on November 3, 1916, the Dodge brothers sued Henry Ford.

The suit was not settled until October 1917. The Michigan Superior Court agreed that Ford had the right to pursue corporate expansion. However, the court declared that "Any corporation is organized to carry on primarily for the profit of the stockholders." The court said that the Ford Motor Company had enough money to both undertake expansion and pay dividends. Of the $20.8 million the court ordered the company to pay out, some $2 million would go to the Dodge brothers.

While Henry Ford grudgingly doled out the $20.8 million, some $12 million to himself (he being the largest stockholder), the industrialist was furious. Ford was now prepared to do anything he could to get rid of the other stockholders—once and for all.

Though Henry Ford had no intention of actually doing so, he threatened, publicly, to form a new company, one that would build a stripped-down, cheaper car. In doing so, Ford scared the remaining stockholders into selling out to him. Such a new company would, it was assumed, drive the current Ford Motor Company out of business.

The scheme worked, though it cost Henry Ford $105.8 million. But now Ford, his wife Clara, and his son Edsel were the sole owners of the Ford Motor Company. The company Henry Ford founded in 1903 was finally "all in the family."

The four o'clock shift change at the Ford Motor Company Highland Park plant, sometime between 1910 and 1920.

Library of Congress LC-DIG-det-4a25685

39

PACIFISTS AND WARMONGERS

ON JULY 28, 1914, the world went to war. Before it was over on November 11, 1918, 10 million soldiers would die and twice that many would be injured. What was called the Great War, later known as World War I, was fought primarily in Europe. The United States would not enter the conflict until April 6, 1917.

Henry Ford was against America's participation in the war from the start. He spoke out in opposition to what was then called **preparedness**, a country's gathering of arms for a fight. "I don't believe in preparedness," Ford declared. "It's like a man carrying a gun. Men and nations who carry guns get into trouble. If I had my way, I'd throw every ounce of gunpowder into the sea and strip soldiers of their insignias."

Ford was a **pacifist**, one who is opposed to war and seeks peace. Acting on his pacifism, in December 1915 Henry Ford sought to achieve European peace through **mediation**. He chartered (hired) a steamship to take him and a large group of peace delegates to Norway, at the time a neutral country. Once there, they would attempt to settle the conflict.

Eleven days before his ship, named the *Oscar II*, departed from New York Harbor, Ford invited the press to his hotel room in lower Manhattan. Nervously and awkwardly, Ford began,

"Well boys, we've got a ship."

"What ship, Mr. Ford?"

"Why, the *Oscar II*."

"Well, what about her? What are you going to do with her?"

"Why, we're going to Europe to stop the war."

"Stop the *war*?"

"Yes, we're going to have the boys out of the trenches by Christmas. The main idea is to crush militarism and get the boys out of the trenches. Our objective is to stop war for all times and also preparedness. War is nothing but preparedness. No boy would ever kill a bird if he didn't have a sling-shot or a gun."

On December 5, 1915, the *Oscar II*, dubbed the "Peace Ship," left New York, bound for the German submarine–infested waters of the North Atlantic.

What Ford said about having men out of the trenches by Christmas received much attention—and ridicule. Trenches there were plenty of. If the length of the zigzagging ditches of both sides were added up, they would stretch around the world—25,000 miles. Getting soldiers out of these trenches and home would be a tall order.

As the *Oscar II* made its way to Europe, newspaper cartoons back home made fun of Ford and his peace expedition. One showed Henry Ford waving a sign that said PEACE. Another showed an erupting volcano labeled WAR, while Ford stood on a nearby peak shaking his fist and yelling, NOW YOU STOP!

Despite the criticism, Ford plunged ahead.

Yet in the end the expedition was a failure. Ford himself became violently ill on the last leg of the trip. A day after the *Oscar II* docked in Norway, Henry Ford turned around and headed back to the United States, leaving the remaining delegates to do what little they could.

By the time the industrialist arrived home, the press, which had been vicious in its judgment, began to change its tune. Regardless of what anyone thought of Henry Ford, a private citizen, trying to stop the war, many admired his sincerity and effort. The *New York American* argued that Ford "Deserves respect, not ridicule. If America's political leaders had put forth one-tenth the individual effort that Henry Ford put forth, the boys would have been out of the trenches by Christmas."

Henry Ford himself said of his peace mission, "I do not regret the attempt. The mere fact that it failed is not, to me, conclusive proof that it was not worth trying. We learn more from our failures than from our successes."

EAGLE BOATS FOR UNCLE SAM

ON FEBRUARY 3, 1917, the United States broke off all relations with Germany. Two days later, Henry Ford announced, "In the event of a declaration of war, I will place our factory at the disposal of

President Woodrow Wilson at Preparedness Parade in 1916.
Library of Congress LC-DIG-hec-07138

the United States government and will operate without one cent of profit." It took less than a month for Henry Ford to go from active pacifist to war manufacturer. The industrialist stated, "If militarism can be crushed only with militarism... I am in on it to the finish."

In support of American efforts to win the Great War, Henry Ford quickly got busy. By the time the war ended in 1918, the Ford Motor Company had produced 39,000 cars, ambulances, and trucks for American and Allied forces. Ford produced 34,000 tractors for British and American farmers. Furthermore, 3,940 Liberty motors for aircrafts, with 415,377 cylinders, were produced. Ford was just gearing up to manufacture tanks when the war ended.

The biggest war contract that Henry Ford secured from the government, however, was to build submarine patrol vessels, known as Eagles. The navy needed a special ship that would search out and destroy German U-boats (submarines).

On January 17, 1918, the secretary of the navy sent Ford an order for 100 boats at $275,000 each. A whole new facility, 1,700 feet long, 350 feet wide, and 100 feet tall, had to be built to take on the project. The building was big enough for three production lines, each capable of accommodating seven boats.

Building Eagle boats turned out to be a lot more challenging than turning out cars, however. For one thing, cars are assembled using bolts. Boats are put together with rivets or through casting. The Ford workforce, which reached 8,000 at its peak, had difficulty adjusting to the new techniques necessary to build the boats. The project stalled time and time again.

When an Eagle boat was finished, it would be launched directly into the water, sliding down a bank on rollers, and tested. Then, according to Douglas Brinkley,

Each boat made a shakedown cruise via the Detroit River to Lake Erie, executing hairpin turns

The "Peace Ship," *Oscar II*, of the Holland America Line, that took Henry Ford and a delegation of peace advocates to Norway in 1915. Library of Congress LC-USZ62-71920

THERE ARE MANY CAUSES you might consider promoting. Fighting breast cancer, heart disease, and childhood obesity are just a few health-related causes. Preventing drunk driving, promoting voting in school elections, and protesting school bullying are a few more ideas. The opportunities are endless.

In late 1915, Henry Ford chartered the *Oscar II* as his "Peace Ship." It left New York Harbor in early December, taking a group of pacifists to Europe. Everything was done in such haste that no one thought to design a Peace Ship flag or banner. In this activity, you design and fabricate a flag, banner, streamer, pennant, or other emblem to publicize a cause you care deeply about.

You'll Need
- Pencil (with eraser)
- Poster board
- Colored pencils, crayons, or markers
- Construction paper, various colors
- Scissors
- Glue
- Embellishments such as beads, sequins, ribbons, tiny trinkets, bottle caps, etc.

1. Before you begin, spend time thinking about what your flag will look like. Be aware of the common symbols for your cause, such as a flower for peace, a pink ribbon for breast cancer awareness, and a ballot for voting. You might want to include written quotes on your emblem. One possible design for an antiwar poster is shown below. On the left is an illustration of trench warfare, a brutal fighting strategy used during World War I. On the right is a conference table showing representatives sitting down to negotiate a peace agreement.

2. Sketch an outline of your emblem on the poster board. Use a pencil so you can alter your design until you're happy with it.

3. Use colored pencils, crayons, or markers to add color. You can also cut out shapes from construction paper and glue them on your banner. Put the finishing touches on your emblem by decorating with beads, sequins, ribbons, or other embellishments.

Your teacher may want you to stand up in class and present your flag or banner. Describe what the design means to you.

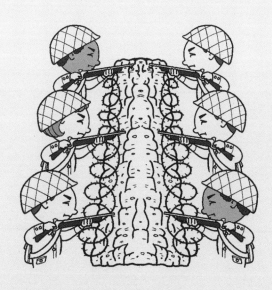

and other maneuvers meant to break the craft and everything on it, if possible. Clerk George Brown remembered that many of the Highland Park office personnel were invited as a courtesy on the shakedown cruises, but "some of them would come back and stay home a week, seasick!"

In the end, just 60 Eagle boats were built. Although they were considered quite seaworthy, only one of the boats actually went into service before the war ended.

The Ford Motor Company's reputation suffered with the Eagle boat project. It seems Henry Ford, in his eagerness to help the war effort, had simply promised too much. After all, while building Eagle boats, Ford was turning out not only tractors and airplane engines but Model Ts as well. Even with reduced car production, the Ford Motor Company assembled 50,000 Model T automobiles in 1918. The navy, however, did not ask Ford to build ships for them again.

PATRIOTIC DUTY

IN JUNE 1917, President Woodrow Wilson called Henry Ford to Washington. "Mr. Ford," the president began, "we are living in very difficult times—times when men must sacrifice themselves for their country." What concession the president wanted from Ford was for the industrialist to run for the US Senate from Michigan in the 1918 election. If Ford won, the reasoning went, the president would have the crucial support he needed for his postwar peace policies.

Ford was reluctant to heed Wilson's request. Nonetheless, he saw the president's appeal as a patriotic duty. Ford would run, but strictly on his own terms.

To begin with, Henry Ford, now 55 years old, made clear his distaste for active campaigning. "If

One of many Eagle submarine chasers built by Henry Ford (1918). Wikimedia Commonsa

the people of Michigan choose to elect me to that office, I would accept it," Ford declared. "But I will not lift a finger to bring it about."

Many of Ford's friends found his entry into politics baffling. "What do you want to do that for?" asked Thomas Edison. "You can't speak. You wouldn't say a damned word. You'd be mum."

"I have made only one speech in my life," Ford confessed. "It was at Sing Sing Prison in New York, to thirteen hundred prisoners. I got stage fright

A World War I memorial in Jackson, Mississippi.
Library of Congress LC-DIG-highsm-04690 (photographer: Carol M. Highsmith)

The Great War

IT WAS CALLED THE GREAT WAR (1914 TO 1918) because more than 17 million people lost their lives. When an even greater war began 20 years later (1939 to 1945), 60 million people died. The Great War then became known as World War I. The second war is referred to as World War II.

The causes of World War I are complex. Historians debate the issue to this day. The immediate cause, however, is clear. It involved the assassination of the Austrian archduke Franz Ferdinand on June 28, 1914, in Sarajevo, Bosnia. The assassin was a 19-year-old Bosnian revolutionary named Gavrilo Princip. Ferdinand's assassination was the trigger that set in motion declarations of war involving numerous European countries.

The key to so many countries becoming involved was the establishment of defense alliances. An alliance is an agreement between two or more countries to come to each other's aid if one of them is attacked. Before

World War I began, Russia and Serbia were allied. So were Germany and Austria-Hungary. France had an alliance with Russia. Britain, France, and Belgium were also in alliance. Finally, Japan was an ally of Britain. It was a complicated affair.

When Austria-Hungary declared war on Serbia, Russia got involved to defend Serbia. Germany then declared war on Russia. France was then drawn in against Germany and Austria-Hungary. When Germany attacked France through Belgium, Britain was pulled into the fighting. That meant Japan would have to enter the war. Later, Italy and the United States would join the combat.

Given the tangle just described, it is not surprising that many Americans, including Henry Ford, felt their country should stay out of the confused European conflict, known then as the Great War.

EYELETS AS RIVETS

THE EAGLE BOATS HENRY FORD BUILT were riveted, not bolted, together. A rivet is a headed pin that is passed through a hole in two pieces of metal that are to be joined. The plain end of the rivet is then smashed down so as to make a second head. In this activity, you will become a "riveter" using craft eyelets.

You'll Need

⚙ Card stock, any color

⚙ Scissors

⚙ Eyelet setting mat, 4 inches by 4 inches (10.2 centimeters by 10.2 centimeters), available at most hobby or arts and crafts stores; a piece of cardboard, ⅛-inch (3.2-millimeter) thick, would also work

⚙ Eyelet setting tool, available at most hobby or arts and craft stores

⚙ Hammer

⚙ Package of eyelets, ³⁄₁₆ inch (4.8 millimeter), available at most hobby or arts and crafts stores

1. Cut two pieces of card stock, each approximately 3 inches by 3 inches (7.6 centimeters by 7.6 centimeters), and place them (one on top of the other) on top of the setting mat.

2. Select the correct setting tool attachment that will make the right size hole in both pieces of card stock to accommodate an eyelet.

3. Place the setting tool in the position you want to make the hole. Using the hammer, pound on top of the setting tool enough times to make a hole through both pieces of card stock.

4. Holding both pieces of card stock together, insert an eyelet and flip the card stock over.

5. Select the correct setting tool attachment for setting the eyelet.

6. Place the setting tool in position over the eyelet. Using the hammer, pound on top of the setting tool until the back of the eyelet splits and flattens.

7. Repeat steps 2 through 7 to practice "riveting." Your eyelets are holding two pieces of card stock together just like rivets do with metal. You might set your "rivets" to create a fun pattern, such as a happy face.

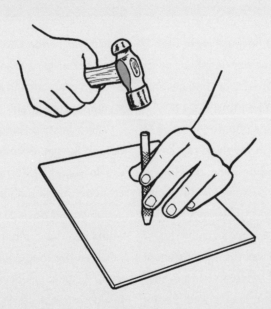
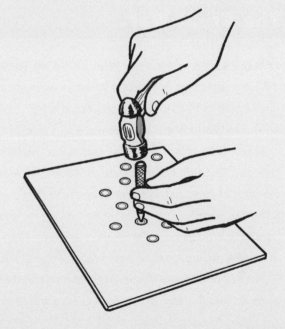

and all I could think of to say was, 'I am glad to see so many of you here.'"

Ford's poor public speaking skills and refusal to spend money were not his only handicaps in the Senate race. Among other factors, there was the issue of Edsel's draft deferment during the war.

Henry Ford's Republican opponent, Truman Newberry, was quick to question Edsel's refusal to serve in World War I. Edsel, Ford's only son, was 24 years old when the United States entered the war. Though Edsel would later claim he wanted to serve, his father used his influence in Washington to have his son deferred. He had Edsel appeal to the draft board claiming exemption on the grounds that he would be of greater service to the country working at the Ford Motor Company. Edsel never went to war.

When votes were counted, Henry Ford received 212,487 to Truman Newberry's 220,054. Ford immediately demanded a recount. In the final tally, Ford lost the election by only 4,337 votes. If Henry Ford had made at least some effort to persuade the voting citizens of his state that he was their person for the Senate, he probably would have been elected to the upper chamber of the US Congress.

Ford was not a good loser. He claimed that Newberry had spent more money in winning than Michigan election law permitted. Ford was sure that the big money interests on Wall Street were behind Newberry's success. "If they would spend $176,000 to win a single Senate seat," he told an associate, "we may be certain that they would spend $176,000,000 to get control of the country."

Though a reluctant candidate from the start, it seems Henry Ford grew to like the limelight his Senate campaign had bathed him in. In 1922, the industrialist allowed his name to be bandied about for president. The idea went nowhere.

Even though Ford failed in his Senate bid, his running demonstrated his general appeal among voters, especially in the Midwest. Henry Ford was seen by many as the honest reformer who promised to clean things up.

Yet, by entering the political arena, Ford displayed a naive, amateurish side that just as many individuals found disturbing. By war's end, Henry Ford was seen as the man who could produce cars for sale at home or for the war effort. But when he strayed from such activity, into peace and politics, Ford was clearly off his mark.

This cartoon plays off the popular 1923 song "Yes, We Have No Bananas!" and shows Ford hesitant to jump into the "presidential contest pool."

U.S. Senate Collection, Center for Legislative Archives

⚙

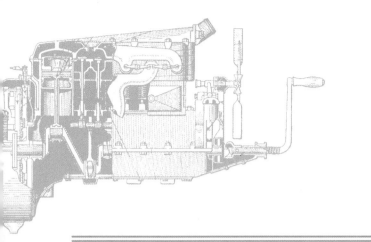

5

ON THE DARK SIDE

In 1916 the United States and Mexico almost went to war. The Mexican revolutionary Pancho Villa's raids across the Rio Grande were becoming unacceptable to those Americans in the border region. In response, President Woodrow Wilson called in the National Guard.

When a reporter from the *Chicago Tribune* asked Henry Ford, the pacifist, whether employees of the Ford Motor Company selected to serve in the Guard would be fired as a result, the company's secretary treasurer, Frank Klingensmith, spoke up, saying something to the effect that this was true. On June 22, 1916, the *Chicago Tribune* carried the story, stating (incorrectly) that, "Ford employees who volunteered to bear arms for the U.S. will lose their jobs."

Henry Ford circa 1919.
Wikimedia Commons

The next day, the *Tribune* printed an editorial that declared, "If Ford allows this rule of his shops to stand he will reveal himself not merely an *ignorant* idealist but an *anarchistic* enemy of the nation which protects him in his wealth." On June 25, Henry Ford sued for **libel**, asking for $1 million in damages.

Nearly three years later, on May 12, 1919, the case went to trial. By that time, the *Tribune* had more or less dropped the accusation that Ford was an **anarchist**. Instead, it hoped to defend what it had printed three years earlier, stating that Ford was an ignorant man and an idealist whose views on preparedness had endangered the country during the Great War. Ford, in turn, claimed that the editorial had "sought to bring the **plaintiff** [Ford] into public hatred, contempt, ridicule, and financial injury."

The trial was held in the tiny town of Mount Clemens, Michigan, since no impartial jury could be found in either Detroit or Chicago.

The *Tribune*, led by its 35-year-old publisher, Robert McCormick, retained nine lawyers. The legal team immediately hired an entire law firm to pretend it was the Ford team of lawyers. The idea was for the *Tribune*'s team to figure out the possible strategy of its opponent.

For his part, Henry Ford had eight lawyers and a group of 63 attendants. Ford established his own news bureau. Not trusting the big-city newspapers, the Ford legal team sought to distribute daily summaries of the proceedings to hundreds of small-town papers. They felt such publications would be more likely to support Ford's position. By the time the trial opened, with dozens of reporters on hand, the whole affair promised to erupt into a media circus.

TRIVIA ON TRIAL

FORD'S LAWYERS knew the *Tribune*'s council would go after their client on the issue of his supposed ignorance. Ford's team tried to coach him ahead of time. The lead Ford lawyer, Alfred Lucking, found Ford a most unwilling pupil.

When his history lesson began, Ford wandered over to a window and observed, "Say, that airplane is flying pretty low, isn't it?" Then, gently, the student would be brought back to his seat. A few minutes later, it began again. "Look at that bird there, pretty little fellow, isn't it?" Ford would announce. The head of the Ford Motor Company simply could not concentrate on what he felt was merely trivia. Ford's attorneys finally threw up their hands in frustration.

Henry Ford was placed on the witness stand for eight grueling days of examination as to whether or not he was an uneducated man. Elliot Stevenson, head council for the *Tribune*, questioned Ford's knowledge of American history—the history any schoolchild supposedly should have known.

Q: *Have there been any revolutions in this country?*
A: *Yes.*
Q: *When?*
A: *In 1812.*
Q: *One in 1812, eh? Any other time?*
A: *I don't know of any others.*
Q: *Do you know that this country was born in a revolution?*
A: *Yes, in 1776.*
Q: *Did you forget that revolution?*
A: *I guess so.*
Q: *Do you know what forced us into the Revolutionary War?*
A: *No, I do not.*

It only got worse.

When Stevenson asked Ford to read something, the manufacturer said he had left his glasses at home. Stevenson suggested to Ford that if he chose not to read anything in court, it might leave the impression that Henry Ford could not read at all. "Do you want to leave it that way?" the attorney asked. Ford answered, "Yes, you can leave it that way. I am not a fast reader and I have the hay fever, and I would make a botch of it."

In the end, Ford had to admit, "I don't like to read books; they muss up my mind."

The entire testimony aside, it would be wrong to conclude that Henry Ford came out of his court ordeal looking like a total buffoon. His unassum-

ing responses to questions gained him wide approval from ordinary people. Ford demonstrated a gift for simple, down-to-earth speech. When Stevenson went after him yet again, asking, "What was the United States originally?" Ford answered, "Land, I guess."

After further questions of this type, Ford, in a rare moment of fluster, turned to his opponent.

Henry Ford had a gift for folksy speech. He once commented that "if you chop your own wood you will warm yourself twice." Ford is doing just that in this 1921 photograph. Library of Congress LC-DIG-npcc-04715

VISIT AN AUTOMOBILE MUSEUM

THERE ARE MORE than 100 museums dedicated to celebrating American automobiles. These are fascinating places that display classic automobiles of every description, many in pristine condition. Car museums have a wealth of programs devoted to educating young and old about the role and influence of the automobile in America. Whether you chose to visit an automobile museum with your family or as a field trip with your school, you are sure to enjoy the experience.

You'll Need

⚙ Computer with Internet access

⚙ Notebook

⚙ Pencil

⚙ Sketchbook (optional)

⚙ Camera (optional)

1. Visit the National Association of Automobile Museums (NAAM) at www.naam.museum, where you will find information on more than 100 automobile museums in the United States. Follow the instructions to locate a museum near you. Once you have selected a museum, explore its website. See if you can arrange a visit with your family or school.

2. Upon arrival at the museum, gather any free literature the museum has to offer. See if there are any Ford cars on display, particularly Model Ts and Model As. Check out the competition, the cars that competed with Fords, particularly with the Model T, from 1908 to 1927. Note that while the Model T changed little in its 19-year history, many other car manufacturers were producing exciting and competitive vehicles. As you walk around, think about how the automobile has impacted American life and culture. Jot down your thoughts and observations in your notebook.

3. If you brought a sketchbook along, sketch the car that most interests you. If you have a camera, take pictures (if allowed) of interesting automobiles.

4. Note how simple the early automobile dashboards were. Why do you suppose this was the case? Note the standard equipment on most early cars, those from around 1900 to 1930. How does such equipment compare with today's automobiles? Note how car body styles changed over the decades, from boxier in the early years to more streamlined later on. What do you think explains the change?

5. Visit the museum store. Have fun!

"I could find a man in five minutes who could tell me all about it."

After 14 weeks of testimony, the case finally went to the jury. Twelve jurors found in favor of Henry Ford. Ford, they said, had in fact been libeled. He was awarded a token amount for damages of six cents.

Though intellectuals felt Ford had embarrassed himself to no end, ordinary people had come to a different verdict. In the words of the *Fairbury* [Nebraska] *Journal*, "A few less smart-aleck attorneys and a few more Henry Fords, and the world would have less trouble and more to eat."

Ford, though humbled in some ways, found that the Mount Clemens trial had actually improved his status—as a man of the people.

"THE INTERNATIONAL JEW"

ON MAY 22, 1920, the *Dearborn Independent* weekly ran a front-page editorial with the shrill caption, THE INTERNATIONAL JEW: THE WORLD'S PROBLEM. "There is a race," the editorial stated, "a part of humanity, which has never yet been received as a welcome part. This people has ever been fouling the earth and plotting to dominate it.... This racial problem is the 'prime' question confronting all society."

The *Dearborn Independent*, which called itself the "Chronicle of the Neglected Truth," was owned by Henry Ford.

Though the industrialist never actually wrote a word that appeared in the *Independent*, the **ghostwriter** who did, William J. Cameron, accurately reflected Ford's views. And the **anti-Semitic** (anti-Jewish) poison that Cameron wrote would appear in the next 91 consecutive issues of the *Dearborn Independent*, reaching hundreds of thousands of readers. At its high point, the paper boasted a circulation of 650,000.

Throughout its long run, the *Independent* would simply not give up on blaming the Jews for the world's problems. Cameron and his staff accused American Jews, a cultural group with the lowest crime rate in the nation, of being "vile, lewd, nasty, erotic, and criminal." The Jews were faulted for tempting Americans with liquor. They were called "the 'skunk-cabbage of American jazz,' and the 'corrupters' of professional baseball."

Why? Why did Henry Ford choose to attack the Jews, to go after them in such a hateful, spiteful way? In doing so, the manufacturer, so respected in many other aspects of his long and accomplished life, would ruin his reputation for the rest of his days—and well beyond. To this day, there are those who will not buy a Ford product in spite of the Ford Motor Company's sincere and significant efforts to make up for its founder's anti-Semitism.

There is little evidence that Henry Ford, growing up as he did in a rural, farming environment, ever actually met a Jewish person as a boy. Nor is there a record of his family ever having a negative encounter with a Jewish person.

It is true that the white-hooded Ku Klux Klan, a bigoted, nativist organization (favoring the people native to an area rather than immigrants or perceived outsiders) that opposed blacks and Jews, had a long and successful rise in the state of Michigan. By 1920, when the *Dearborn Independent* was about to launch its attack on Jewish people, the Klan had 875,000 members in the state—the largest group in the United States. The Klan was well populated by many in the Detroit area, including some in high places.

It seems, however, that Ford's long-standing distrust of bankers, financiers, and Wall Street investors played a vital role in his hostility toward the Jews. "I would tear down my plants, brick by brick, with my own hands, before I would let Wall Street get a hold of them," Ford once proclaimed.

And who were these Wall Street money men? Ford believed that a disproportional number were Jewish. It is this correlation that Ford insisted on between financiers and Jews that many claim best explains the roots of the man's hatred for the Jews.

"HAS SOMETHING COME BETWEEN US?"

JEWS HAVE been persecuted for their religious beliefs for more than 3,000 years. Yet anti-Semitism is a relatively new term. It was coined by Wilhelm

Wall Street in the early 1900s. Henry Ford was very mistrustful of Wall Street bankers, investors, and financiers.

Library of Congress Prints and Photographs Division LC-B2- 4125-7

54

Marr, a German, in 1879. With anti-Semitism, Marr went beyond traditional Jew-hating on religious grounds to a new ideology based on a belief that Jewish people made up a separate "nation," culture, and even "race." The Jewish "race," Marr argued, was taking over his beloved Germany by achieving great success in the professions, in the arts, and in business, particularly in banking. With anti-Semitism, Marr insisted, good Christians could detest ethnic Jews not only on religious terms, but for cultural and economic reasons as well.

Henry Ford felt that anti-Semitism gave him full license to take on the Jewish population—on Marr's terms. Week after week, the *Independent*'s nasty essays, all reflecting Henry Ford's convictions, continued. The titles of individual articles tell the story:

THE JEW IN CHARACTER AND BUSINESS

DOES JEWISH POWER CONTROL
THE WORLD PRESS?

HOW JEWS IN THE U.S. CONCEAL
THEIR STRENGTH

JEWISH DEGRADATION OF
AMERICAN BASEBALL

JEWISH JAZZ BECOMES OUR
NATIONAL MUSIC

HOW JEWISH INTERNATIONAL
FINANCE FUNCTIONS

The last essay of the long-running series on "The International Jew" offered a veiled threat. Entitled

An Address to Gentiles on the Jewish Problem, it spelled out what one might do to curb Jewish influence in the United States. The composition, according to Steven Watts, "urged vigilant citizens to open their eyes to Jewish subversion and stop it peacefully but firmly."

Ford's bigotry toward the Jews was extreme. Informed that brass was a "Jew metal," the industrialist insisted that it never be used in his Model T automobiles. Engineers responded by utilizing it wherever necessary, then covering it up with black paint.

Many people were appalled by Henry Ford's crusade. In early 1921, more than 100 prestigious Americans—from former president Woodrow Wilson to Cardinal William O'Connell—signed a statement condemning Ford's essays.

Surprisingly, Henry Ford did have a few Jewish associates and friends. Albert Kahn, the leading industrial architect of his time, designed both the Ford Motor Company's Highland Park plant and an even bigger factory to come, the Rouge. Kahn was Jewish.

Then there was Rabbi Leo M. Franklin, a neighbor of Ford's. Each year, Henry Ford gave Franklin a **custom-built** Model T. After the *Dearborn Independent*'s anti-Semitic articles began running, the rabbi returned the latest Model T given to him. Ford, surprised, telephoned Franklin. Incredibly, the manufacturer asked, "What's wrong, Dr. Franklin? Has something come between us?"

"DEEPLY MORTIFIED"

When it came to the Jews, Henry Ford was to yet again find himself in a place he most detested—a court of law.

On the night of March 31, 1927, Henry Ford, driving his Ford **coupe** down Michigan Avenue

A Hoax of Hate

A DOCUMENT CALLED "THE PROTOCOLS [AN ORIGINAL DRAFT] of the Elders of Zion, or 'The Jewish Program to Conquer the World'" is an anti-Semitic hoax. First published in Russia in 1903, "The Protocols" describes a supposed Jewish plan for world domination and claims to document the minutes of a late 19th-century meeting of Jewish leaders. At the gathering, "The Protocols" asserted, such leaders discussed ways to subvert the morals of Christians. Furthermore they allegedly plotted to gain control of the press and the world economy.

According to the document's author, Hermann Goedsche, writing under the name Sir John Retcliffe, a secret conference of rabbis would meet every 100 years to review the past 100 years and to make plans for the next century.

"The Protocols of the Elders of Zion" is a hoax. No such conference ever took place. The document's sole purpose is to spread anti-Semitism throughout the world.

Tragically, to a considerable extent the document achieved its purpose. Adolf Hitler and the Nazis publicized the text as though it were valid. After the Nazi Party came to power in Germany in 1933, it ordered the text to be used in all German classrooms. Some historians have suggested that Hitler used "The Protocols" as his primary justification for the Holocaust, Hitler's plan to annihilate Jews during World War II.

Henry Ford had 500,000 copies of "The Protocols of the Elders of Zion" printed and distributed throughout the United States in the 1920s. He later apologized for doing so, and he admitted to "The Protocols" being a forgery.

DISASSEMBLE AND REASSEMBLE ANYTHING

TAKING SOMETHING (a toy, for example) apart can be quite easy. Putting it back together is another matter. To be successful at reassembly, you need a method to identify the order in which you remove parts, components, and screws and nuts. You need to know what was removed first, second, third, and so on. You then work backward, reassembling the last item first, then the next to the last item, and so forth.

In this activity, you disassemble and then reassemble a toy using the "clock-coding" method. Mechanics working with automobiles, from the earliest times to the present, have used this method to make sure what they take apart can be put back together. As you go through life, you will find many uses of the clock-coding method to disassemble and reassemble almost anything.

You'll Need

⚙ Drawing compass

⚙ Pencil

⚙ White paper

⚙ A toy or other object to be taken apart—not too complicated but not too simple

⚙ Assortment of tools for disassembly and reassembly (screwdrivers, pliers, wrenches, etc.)

1. Using the drawing compass, draw a circle at least 6 inches (15.2 centimeters) in diameter on a sheet of paper.

2. Label the circle 1 through 12, like the face of a clock.

3. Start disassembling your object. As you remove the first part (probably a screw), set it at the one o'clock position. Jot down a note to identify where the part came from.

4. Proceeding clockwise, place the next part removed at two o'clock. Continue like this until you have disassembled your toy as far as you want. (If there are more than 12 parts to be taken off, you can label the clock face with a 13 starting at the one o'clock position. Place the 13th part farther out from the clock where the part for one o'clock is positioned so you don't get the two confused. Advance like this as far as necessary.

5. After disassembly, start the reassembly process. Proceed backward from the last point on the clock until the toy is reassembled.

toward his country estate, was sideswiped by a big Studebaker touring car with two men it. At least that is what the industrialist later claimed. Ford's Model T lumbered down a 15-foot embankment and hit a tree a few feet from the Rouge River. Dazed and bleeding, Ford managed to stagger home. Two days later he was taken to the hospital.

When an aide to Henry Ford, Harry Bennett, assured his boss, "I'm going to find out who knocked you into the river if it takes me the rest of my life," Ford demurred. "Now you just drop this," he told Bennett. "Probably it was a bunch of kids."

Some have suggested that Ford faked the accident in order to avoid appearing in court involving another lawsuit. Back in 1924, the *Dearborn Independent*, in its continued assault on Jewish citizens, had gone personal. The paper's target was a young Jewish lawyer named Aaron Sapiro. Sapiro worked to organize farm cooperatives throughout the country. The *Independent* characterized his attempts "as a plot by Jewish international finan-

ciers to capture control of the American economy." Sapiro sued Henry Ford and the Dearborn Publishing Company (owners of the *Dearborn Independent*) for $1 million, claiming defamation of character.

Rather than face a lengthy, exposing trial once again, Ford settled out of court with Sapiro. On December 31, 1927, Ford ordered the *Dearborn Independent* to quit publishing altogether. As part of his settlement, Henry Ford issued a formal apology six months later. In it, he stated that he was "deeply mortified that his journal, which is intended to be constructive and not destructive, has been made the medium for resurrecting exploded fictions." Ford went on to say, "I am fully aware of the virtues of the Jewish people as a whole." Ford asked for forgiveness.

Forgiveness was granted by some, but not by others. For his part, Henry Ford would refrain from publicly attacking the Jewish people for the rest of his life.

⚙

Henry Ford and son
Edsel sit in the rare
Model F Ford, 1905.
© Corbis

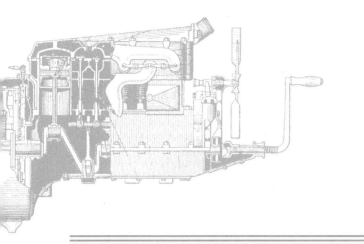

FATHER AND SONS

"**H**enry Ford's greatest achievement was changing the face of America and putting the world on wheels," Charles Sorensen, a high-ranking executive with the Ford Motor Company, once said. "His greatest failure was his treatment of his only son, Edsel."

It did not begin that way; a more doting father would be hard to find.

Edsel was born on November 6, 1893, the year his father turned 30. Henry lavished attention on his son, spending hours playing with him, and seeing to it that hundreds of pictures were taken with the two together. In his childhood years, Edsel proved to be an alert and obedient son. The boy worshiped his father as he grew and became a man, until the day he died in 1943, four years before Henry Ford passed away.

At the age of eight, Edsel was given his own car. There being no minimum driving age at the time, the third grader drove his "buggy" to and from school.

Edsel received excellent marks in school, rarely getting anything less than a B+. Though he worked hard at all his subjects and paid close attention while in class, his notebooks were filled with sketches of automobiles. From an early age, Edsel showed an advanced artistic ability.

Upon completing high school, Edsel had every intention of going to college. His father, never much for formal education, had another idea. Edsel reluctantly agreed to go straight to work—at the Ford Motor Company.

When Edsel turned 21, his father drove him to a Detroit bank. "I have a million in gold deposited here," Ford told a vice president. "This is Edsel's birthday and I want him to have it." Money would never be Edsel Ford's problem.

As Edsel moved up the ladder at the Ford Motor Company, he earned his associates' admiration. They saw him as considerate, respectful, and low-key. "He was well-liked by everybody," said engineer William C. Klann. "He was what you would call a gentleman."

Edsel Ford, circa 1921, not long after becoming president of the Ford Motor Company.
Library of Congress LC-USZ62-83073

At age 22, Edsel became a member of the Ford Motor Company's board of directors. The year was 1915. The following year Edsel married Eleanor Clay in a union of wealth and society.

It was clear that Ford's son was destined for the top job at the Ford Motor Company. On January 1, 1919, at the unbelievably young age of 25, Edsel became the company's president, a title he held for the rest of his life.

While Edsel sat in the president's chair, his father remained close by. Indeed, Henry Ford had put his son in the leadership position as part of a **stock** manipulation scheme. Though technically in the background, the elder Ford continued to run the company. Henry Ford made all the major decisions. It was his company.

Car styling, a new concept in itself, was something Edsel took a keen interest in. "As cars became more complex and as competition to the Model T increased," Robert Lacey, author of *Ford: The Men and the Machine*, observed, "the look of an automobile was to become one of the key ingredients of its success." Edsel planned to be closely involved in any new Ford car designs.

THE LINCOLN MOTOR COMPANY

ON FEBRUARY 6, 1922, the headline in the *New York Times* proclaimed, MRS. FORD, THROUGH

SYMPATHY, URGED $8,000,0000 PURCHASE OF LINCOLN MOTORS. On February 12, the *Times* confirmed, FORD PAYS $8,000,000 CHECK; COMPLETES HIS PURCHASE OF THE LINCOLN MOTOR COMPANY. The buy was a gift to Edsel from his father.

The Lincoln Motor Company was founded in 1917 by Henry Leland and his son Wilfred. The elder Leland was known to be one of the finest engineers in the automotive industry. He was famous for being able to machine an automobile part to an accuracy of 1/100,000 inch. Henry Leland named his new car company after President Abraham Lincoln, a man he greatly admired and for whom he cast his first vote in 1864.

Just five years after the Lincoln Motor Company's birth, it was in serious financial trouble. Henry Ford stepped in and bought the company. Soon after, both Lelands found themselves out of a job. They claimed that Ford promised to leave them in charge. It was not to be. Ford wanted Lincoln for his son.

One would think that Edsel Ford had enough to do running the Ford Motor Company. But when it came to that company, Edsel, the president, had little real authority. The younger Ford saw an opportunity with Lincoln. It would allow him, Edsel felt, the freedom to concentrate on his first love—styling classy automobiles. It was OK with Henry Ford if his son amused himself designing new Lincoln cars.

Those Lincolns would not be for just anyone. They would not be Model Ts. Indeed, Edsel was quoted as declaring, "Father made the most popular car in the world. I would like to make the best car in the world."

Edsel immediately went to work getting rid of the boring, old-fashioned bodies of the Lincoln models. He replaced them with modern, custom-built designs. As a result, Lincoln cars began to sell in larger quantities. In a typical year, 7,000 cars were purchased. True, the Ford Motor Company would turn out that many cars in a single day. But the Lincoln was not competing with the Model T. For Edsel, it was a clear case of quality over quantity.

Though Henry Ford let Edsel go his own way with Lincoln, tensions between father and son began building. Edsel believed the Model T was doomed. With the design innovations he had been introducing at Lincoln, Edsel was eager to include similar changes at the Ford Motor Company. To do so, however, an entirely new car would have to be created. Henry Ford, his support for his beloved Model T as firm as ever, would have none of it.

"THE LITTLE FELLOW"

HENRY FORD's growing displeasure with his son stemmed from a number of issues. The senior Ford did not approve of Edsel's lifestyle. Edsel and his

61

Edsel Ford and his wife, Eleanor Ford, with a Lincoln automobile, around 1922.

From the Collections of the Henry Ford (P.O.833.32571)

wife traveled in different social circles than those of Henry and Clara. Edsel and Eleanor enjoyed living in the elite Detroit suburb of Grosse Pointe. Their friends were at the top of the social pyramid. Henry Ford considered such people snobs and would not socialize with them at all.

But the real problem between father and son was more serious. Henry Ford had grown to believe Edsel was weak and not tough enough to run the Ford Motor Company. As his frustration with his son grew, the elder Ford found many opportunities to humiliate Edsel, often in front of executives and workers. When Edsel drew up plans to have an extension added to the administration building at the Ford factory, Henry objected. Nonetheless, the older Ford let the bulldozers arrive to dig the foundation. Henry then ordered work stopped. He let the hole remain empty for months. It would provide a symbol to all at Ford of the father's authority and the son's disgrace.

In 1919, Henry Ford found a man that would eventually become the tough son he had hoped Edsel could be.

Harry Bennett was 24, the same age as Edsel, when he came to work for the Ford Motor Company. Ford had met him in New York, where he saw the young, aggressive sailor slug it out with a policeman twice his size. Ford admired Bennett's tough-guy persona. He hired him on the spot. Bennett eventually became the boss's eyes and ears at the Ford Motor Company.

Bennett was known as the Little Fellow because he stood only five feet six inches tall. But the man knew no fear. He wore nothing but bow ties because he believed wearing a long tie would give an opponent a handle to steady him in a fight. While on a yacht, Bennett would extend his hand to a guest. He would then push the person off the boat into the water, while laughing hysterically. Bennett kept lions and tigers on the grounds where he lived. Sometimes he would sneak one into the backseat of a visitor's car.

In his basement office at the Ford Motor Company, Bennett stored a gun in his desk drawer. When the Little Fellow got bored with a guest, he would whip out the gun and start firing at a wall target.

Harry Bennett came to acknowledge, "I am Mr. Ford's personal man." In the mid-1920s, Henry Ford made Bennett head watchman at the new Ford plant being developed, known as the Rouge. Bennett would use his new position to build a personal power base that many, particularly Edsel, found hopeless to deal with.

THE ENFORCERS

In a short time, Harry Bennett morphed the watchmen group he created into what became known as the Ford Service Department. Made up of ex-pugs and thugs, these enforcers (800 strong at their peak) roamed the Ford factory instilling fear everywhere they went.

DESIGN AN AUTOMOBILE DASHBOARD

EDSEL FORD WAS THE STYLIST IN THE FORD FAMILY. He was most interested in automobile interiors, particularly the dashboard. The cars Edsel worked on had relatively simple dashboards: a speedometer, an odometer, fuel and temperature gauges, and not much else.

Today, car dashboards are loaded with indicators and instruments. In this activity, you design a dashboard for the car of your dreams. It can be as fanciful and imaginative as you want. It can contain devices that exist today or ones that you imagine might someday come to be, such as voice-activated steering. Let your imagination run wild.

You'll Need

⚙ Cardboard box, approximately 12 inches (30.5 centimeters) on each side.

⚙ Scissors

⚙ Clear tape

⚙ A few sheets of white paper, 8½ inches by 11 inches (21.6 centimeters by 27.9 centimeters)

⚙ Colored pencils, crayons, or markers

⚙ Construction paper, various colors

⚙ Glue stick

⚙ Paper plates, various sizes

⚙ Recycled embellishments, such as beads, tiny trinkets, bottle caps, broken toy parts, lids from jars, dried-up pens and markers, ribbon, old CDs, pictures from catalogs, discarded electronic parts, sewing leftovers, cardboard tubes, plastic packaging from cosmetics, plastic bottles, etc.

1. Prepare your cardboard dashboard base. Using scissors, cut a cardboard box so that it has three main panels. A fourth panel, for the use of a gearshift, cup holder, etc., is also nice.

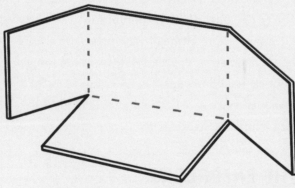

2. Tape together a few sheets of 8½-by-11-inch (21.6-by-27.9-centimeter) paper to use as a guide in laying out your design plan. Write identifying names for each part: steering wheel, gear shift, cell phone holder, radio, rear seat monitor, windshield wipers, horn, etc. You might want to study the family car's dashboard for ideas.

3. Use colored construction paper to cover your cardboard dashboard base. Glue the paper in place.

4. Begin your actual dashboard construction by gluing various size paper plates to the dashboard. They might be used as a tachometer (the dial that shows rotation speed in revolutions per minute, or RPMs), speedometer, clock, fuel gauge, etc.

5. You might cut out images of dashboard parts from catalogs and paste them to your dashboard. Decorate your creation with embellishments, such as bottle caps for radio knobs, and add color using colored pencils, crayons, or markers.

6. Write a brief summary of how various dashboard elements function. Present your dashboard to the class.

Automobile designers do something very similar to what you just did when they create an actual dashboard. It is called a mock-up.

Bennett admired athletes. One summer, he gave jobs to the entire University of Michigan football team as guards and errand boys. Though they may have started out as lowly employees, many moved on to jobs with the Service Department.

In 1926, Ford reduced the workweek from six days to five days. To turn out as many cars in five days as six, the production line had to be sped up.

Pressure increased on every worker. "No one could loaf; he had to keep up with the procession, or the pile-up of stock at his station made it noticeable who was falling behind," wrote Ford biographer Carol Gelderman. "A worker took a bolt and tightened a nut. The wrench was waiting in the raised hand of the next worker. If he lost ten seconds, the machine kept running. He would be left with this bolt and dock in pay. He did this for eight hours."

The effect of the increasingly faster speedup on workers was not hard to imagine. The wife of a General Motors worker told what happened to workers when the line sped up. It could just as easily have been the wife of a Ford man on the line. "You should see my husband come home at night, him and the rest of the men in the buses. So tired like they was dead, and irritable. My husband's a good, kind man. But his children don't dare go near him he's so nervous, and his temper's so bad. And then at night in bed, he shakes, his whole body, he shakes."

Everyone had to keep up the pace. At Ford, a joke went:

"'How did you happen to lose your job?' the new boss asked an applicant who had been fired from the Ford Factory.

'I dropped my monkey wrench one day and by the time I picked it up, I was sixteen cars behind.'"

Workers were given only 15 minutes to eat lunch. During that time, they had to go to the bathroom, wash, and try to eat. Often they would

Henry Ford's head of security, Harry Bennett, left, with Ford in 1939. The former boxer and navy sailor with the tough image was Ford's right-hand man for many years. From the Collections of the Henry Ford (P.833-71965)

THEY CALLED THEMSELVES THE FOUR VAGABONDS [WANDERERS]. Between roughly 1916 and 1921, Henry Ford, Thomas Edison, Harvey Firestone, and John Burroughs set out together on annual summer excursions into the countryside to go camping. One newspaper headlined, MILLIONS OF DOLLARS WORTH OF BRAINS OFF ON VACATION.

While the group may have started out roughing it, each year the trips became less primitive. Eventually, they traveled in a caravan of several luxury cars. Harvey Firestone drove a Pierce-Arrow. Edison rode with Ford in his specially fitted Cadillac touring car, with its built-in kitchen. Cooks, chauffeurs, and photographers added to the party. A dining set that seated 20 was brought along. Each man appeared for breakfast dressed in shirt and tie.

The comforts and formality aside, the Four Vagabonds clearly enjoyed the outings. As one observer commented, "I've never seen a bunch of fellows—you know, big guys with big money—have more fun than they did. They were just like a bunch of kids when they went on these trips."

Henry Ford, President Warren Harding (right of pole), and other notables "roughing" it on one of their camping trips between 1921 and 1923.
Library of Congress LC-DIG-hec-31273 (photographer: Harris & Ewing)

be seen racing back to their stations cramming food in their mouths as they ran.

Bennett's Service Department saw to it that workers kept the speed up. "They checked on men walking around, saw to it that workers did not talk to each other, and enforced the hundred petty regulations of the plant," Gelderman noted. "They were a law unto themselves."

There was no whistling, talking, singing, squatting, or sitting on the job. Even a smile was frowned upon. In response, Ford workers learned to communicate without moving their lips. They developed what became known as the "Ford whisper." Their frozen features were known as the "Fordization of the face."

What, many workers wondered, had become of Henry Ford to allow, indeed, encourage, such treatment? Foremen were, with Bennett's involvement, being picked for their brutality. Ford workers were often fired outright, then rehired at a lower wage; they were no longer proud of what they did to earn a living. Henry Ford once prided himself on the treatment he gave his workers. But he was no longer the man his workers once respected.

In Harry Bennett, Henry Ford got the kind of "son" he claimed he always wanted. In doing so, however, Ford hurt the only true son he had—Edsel. In the process, Henry Ford became a different man. Few welcomed the change.

DESIGN A HUBCAP

WHEEL COVERS HAVE ALWAYS BEEN an important element in automobile design. Such covers began as hubcaps, small metal caps made to cover the center hub of a wooden-spoke wheel and protect it from dust and dirt. In this activity, you design a decorative hubcap. To come up with ideas, you can search the web for hubcap designs, examine photographs of classic cars, or just look more closely at the cars you see every day.

You'll Need

- ⚙ Round paper plate (8½ to 12 inches [21.6 to 30.5 centimeters] in diameter and white on the bottom)
- ⚙ Pencil
- ⚙ Protractor
- ⚙ Recycled embellishments such as beads, bottle caps, broken toy parts, a discarded CD or DVD, buttons, coins, paper clips, hardware (screws, nuts, washers, etc.), staples, poker chips, straws, dots from a hole puncher, and so forth
- ⚙ Glue
- ⚙ Colored pencils, crayons, markers, or paints

1. Before you begin, spend time thinking about what your wheel cover will look like. Use the paper plate (turned over to the white bottom) as a base for the cover.

2. Begin by drawing eight lines radiating from the center of the plate. Use the protractor to space them evenly, 45 degrees apart. These lines will help you space your decorations evenly, just like on a real hubcap.

3. Construct your hubcap using items from your junk drawer or from around your classroom. One idea is to glue a discarded CD to the center of the plate and attach four small binder clips to the CD, spaced evenly.

4. Embellish your hubcap however you like, using your recycled items.

5. Add color to the perimeter of the plate with colored pencils, crayons, markers, or paints.

Given the materials you have on hand, the hubcap you design is limited only by your imagination.

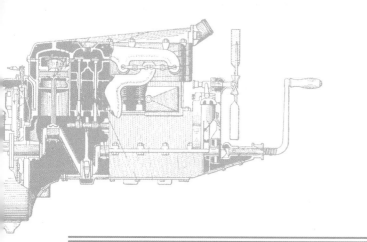

7

FROM SOUP TO NUTS

In 1912, Henry Ford, his wife, and his son took their first trip abroad as a family. In their absence, executives and engineers at the Ford Motor Company worked night and day to provide Ford with a coming-home present— a completely new Model T. When the industrialist returned to the plant, he noticed the car immediately. Ford asked, "What is that over there?"

"Well, Mr. Ford," an employee said, "that's the new car."

"A Ford Car?" Ford enquired.

"Yes, sir."

"How long has that been standing there?"

"Well, about two weeks. They just finished it. It's just going into production."

"It is going into production?"

"Yes, sir. It's all tooled up, the bodies are ordered, and the orders are all placed for that car."

Ford walked around the car three or four times. Then, according to George Brown, an employee who was present at the scene, "Ford took his hands out of his pockets, grabbed hold of a door, and bang—one jerk and he had it off the hinges. He ripped the door off. Then, bang went the other door. Bang went the windshield. He jumped over the back seat and started pounding on the top with the heel of his shoe. He wrecked the car as much as he could, all the while cursing at the top of his lungs."

With the Model T only four years old in 1912, Henry Ford was not about to entertain any ideas concerning its supposed improvement. Ten years later he felt the same way. And five years after that, as late as 1927, when the Model T looked (and acted) like the relic it was, Ford still stubbornly insisted the car should continue being assembled—perhaps forever. The owner of the most successful car company in history considered the Model T his baby. In this instance, change would be very hard for Henry Ford.

Sales figures told first an up, but then a down, story. True, the 10-millionth Model T rolled off the assembly line on June 15, 1924. The 11-millionth Ford came just four months later, in October. To keep that momentum up, Ford was now selling the Model T **runabout** for the unbelievably low price of $260. He made $50 on every car the company sold. For the sales year of 1923–24, the Ford Motor Company earned $100 million.

Yet by 1926, sales were slipping significantly. In that year, deliveries were almost 400,000 units below the previous year's figures. People were buying fewer Model Ts because they were drawn to the competition. Chevrolet, from General Motors (GM), was coming on strong. GM had slashed its price, while loading the Chevrolet with attractive

The first and the 10-millionth Ford, together in 1924.
Library of Congress LC-DIG-det-4a27901

features unavailable on the Model T. In 1926, General Motors sold 730,000 stylish, well-engineered Chevrolets.

In January of that same year, Ernest Kanzler, head of production at Ford, wrote his boss a six-page letter. In it, in the most eloquent and diplomatic manner possible, he said to Henry Ford, "I do not think the Model T will continue to be a satisfactory product to maintain our position in the automobile field." Kanzler urged that the Ford Motor Company, in order to remain competitive—indeed, in order to survive—immediately needed to begin planning for the Model T's replacement. For Kanzler's honesty, Henry Ford fired him eight months later.

"FAREWELL, MY LOVELY"

ASIDE FROM Henry Ford's opposition to replacing the Model T, by 1927 the automobile industry and, more important, the public, sensed that an era was coming to a close. In the end, 15.5 million Model Ts would be sold in the United States. Nearly an additional one million were produced in Canada, and a half million in England. In the 19 years from 1908 to 1927, the Model T accounted for half the automobiles produced in the world.

The Model T's impact was incalculable. The T did more to knit together different parts of the country than any invention up until that time. It turned out to be an earthshaking technology. The

The Ford Motor Company Delivery Department, with 1925 automobiles ready for shipment to dealerships around the country.
Library of Congress LC-USZ62-26766

car satisfied the desire for mobility on a new scale. E. B. White, author of the children's classic *Charlotte's Web*, declared in an article titled, "Farewell, My Lovely," "It [the Model T] was hard-working, commonplace, heroic.... And it was patently [obviously] the sort of thing that could only happen once."

One way to gauge the affection people had for the Model T is to be reminded of the many jokes that fondness spawned. A cartoon from the era depicted one such gag: A grave digger is seen digging a large hole. When asked why the hole is so large, the grave digger replies that it is for a man who asked in his will to be buried in his Model T. The man said the car had pulled him out of every hole, and he was sure it would pull him out of the last.

Jokes aside, times were changing. Roads were being paved all across the country. Cars, as a result, could travel faster and more safely. Even more important, in the last half of the decade the economy was booming. Americans had money to spend. Consumers were ready for more than the Model T offered. They were already transitioning from a simple, practical car to one more attractive and comfortable, with higher performance to boot. The old Model T slogan, "It gets you there and it brings you back," seemed quaint. The Ford Motor Company would have to produce a new car for a more critical customer, or, possibly, see its sales and its profits disappear entirely.

A MATTER OF SURVIVAL

"One sees them all about—men who do not know that yesterday is past, and who woke up this morning with their last year's ideas," wrote Henry Ford in *My Life and Work*. "There is a subtle danger in a man thinking that he is 'fixed' for life. It indicates that the next jolt of the wheel of progress is going to fling him off."

When it came to the Model T, Ford appeared to be the last to listen to his own words. Yet Henry Ford would finally come to see the wisdom of the

advice he gave others. On May 26, 1927, Henry and Edsel Ford drove the 15-millionth Model T out of their factory. Exactly one month later, the *New York Times* declared, "After building 15,000,000 automobiles of one kind Henry Ford is about to begin keeping a new score with a new car. The car is in the making. That much can be said definitely, because Henry Ford himself has announced it."

Indeed, the industrialist had made a complete turnaround. A new Ford, to be known as the Model A, was to be designed and built from scratch. And, as with the Model T, Henry Ford (now age 64) would be involved in every aspect of its creation.

Ford may have been late in coming to the realization that a new car had to be built. But once he did, his true automotive genius came shining through.

Engineer Harold Hicks was awed by the way Henry Ford could get the most out of his staff. Even more, Hicks was amazed at the way Ford cut down development time. Though Henry Ford was not a trained, college-educated engineer, he understood the basic engineering principle of keeping design and fabrication simple. Hicks remembers, "There were too many bolts holding the new **carburetor** together. Henry Ford said to me, 'Cut those bolts down!' I reduced it from 14 little screws down to two bolts. I showed him the design. 'Two is too many!' Ford declared. 'Make it just one bolt!' So the carburetor came out with just a simple bolt down through it."

The Model A would take its inspiration, and many design elements, from the Lincoln automobile that Edsel had developed. The Model A engine would be rated at 40 horsepower—twice that of the Model T. The new car would have **shock absorbers** and rod-operated four-wheel brakes. There would be an automatic windshield wiper, a battery ignition, a speedometer, and gas and oil gauges. The **planetary transmission** of the Model T would be eliminated, to be replaced with a three-speed-with-reverse gearshift. The Model A would have an impressive top speed of 65 miles per hour.

To build such a car, Ford factories had to be completely shut down for rebuilding and retooling. At the Highland Park plant alone, 60,000 workers were laid off for more than six months. The economic impact was felt all over the country. Many suppliers and parts houses went broke. Only the strongest car dealers could survive. With many would-be buyers holding off on a Ford purchase to see what the Model A would be like, salespeople stood around, wringing their hands. It would be half a year more before they could hope to see an actual Model A in their showrooms.

ROUGE RIVER RISING

In 1915, Henry Ford had purchased 2,000 acres of remote land along the Rouge River, a few miles southwest of Detroit. In 1917, he began developing the property into the largest manufacturing facility in the world. Ford wanted the new "superplant," called the Rouge, to be completely self-sufficient. From ore to assembly, or **soup to nuts**, Henry Ford's idea was to achieve "a continuous, nonstop process from raw material to finished product, with no pause even for warehousing or storage."

An air view of the giant Ford Motor Company Rouge River plant, Dearborn, Michigan, probably in 1927.
Library of Congress LC-DIG-det-4a28750

Today, such manufacturing is called **vertical integration**. When the Rouge plant became fully operational in 1928, the first car it assembled was the new Model A.

The final Rouge complex was a mile and a half wide and more than a mile long. There were 93 buildings, totaling 15,767,708 square feet of floor space. More than 120 miles of conveyors transported materials within the factory. A railroad, with 100 miles of track and 16 locomotives, moved

around the property. A bus network crisscrossed 15 miles of paved roads, keeping everything and everyone in constant motion.

According to a history of the Rouge, published by the Ford Motor Company, "There were ore docks, steel furnaces, coke ovens, rolling mills, glass furnaces and plate-glass rollers" at the plant. "Buildings included a tire-making plant, stamping plant, engine casting plant, frame and assembly plant, transportation plant, radiator plant, tool and die plant, and, at one time, even a paper mill. A massive power plant produced enough electricity to light a city the size of nearby Detroit."

At its peak in the 1930s, more than 100,000 workers were employed at the Rouge. A maintenance crew of 5,000 kept the place up to Henry Ford's cleanliness standards.

The idea behind the Rouge was total self-sufficiency. By owning, operating, and coordinating all the resources, Henry Ford believed he could drive down the price of his cars even more. To that end, the company secured forests, iron mines, and limestone quarries throughout Michigan, Minnesota, and Wisconsin. Ford even owned and operated a rubber plantation in Brazil, known as Fordlandia.

Everything at the Rouge was recycled. A soybean processing plant was set up to produce a thousand gallons of oil a day. The oil was then used to make paint; the leftover product went for plastic car parts. The Rouge had its own paper

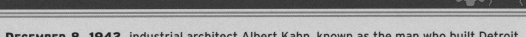

"The Man Who Built Detroit"

ON DECEMBER 8, 1942, industrial architect Albert Kahn, known as the man who built Detroit, died. He was 73 years old.

Kahn, along with many assistants, built more than 2,000 buildings, mostly for the Ford Motor Company and General Motors. According to an obituary in the *New York Times*, "Kahn revolutionized the concept of what a great factory should be: his designs made possible the marvels of modern mass production, and his buildings changed the faces of a thousand cities and towns from Detroit to Novosibirsk [in Russia]."

Albert Kahn's signature development as a designer was the use of reinforced concrete. Such concrete, with its embedded metal rods, was sturdier and less combustible than other materials. Reinforced concrete buildings needed fewer load-bearing walls. As a result, more floor space was freed up for industrial equipment. Albert Kahn's first concrete factory, built for the Packard automobile company, still stands today.

Kahn's buildings were, above all, functional. His first Ford factory, Highland Park, built in 1909, used elevators to spread the assembly of Model Ts over four floors. Huge metal-frame windows allowed for increased lighting and better ventilation.

Kahn is remembered as the architect who built factories for the 20th-century industrial age.

mill, which took in the factory's wastepaper. The result was cardboard for upholstery and wrapping for parts and motors. When pieces were shipped out in wooden boxes, the crates themselves were made at the Rouge. Today, we would call Henry Ford an environmentalist.

When the Model A went into production in 1928, Henry Ford could brag that exactly 28 hours after ore arrived by barge at the Rouge River plant, a finished car would roll off his assembly line.

MODEL A CLAMOR

ON NOVEMBER 28, 1927, Edsel Ford, visiting in New York City, announced that the public would finally get to see the new Ford car. The big event would be held on December 2, at the Fifty-fourth Street branch of a Ford showroom. On the same day of Edsel's announcement, full-page ads were placed in every one of America's 2,000 daily newspapers. The cost to Ford for such advertising was $1.3 million.

On December 2, as promised, the great unveiling took place. The public reaction was astounding. In New York City, more than a quarter million people viewed the Model A in 76 dealer showrooms in the metropolitan district. "The public," the *New York Times* wrote, "gave its approval by signing 50,000 orders."

In Detroit, 100,000 people saw the car displayed on the first day at the city's convention hall. Huge

SET UP A RECYCLING CENTER

WHEN HENRY FORD BUILT the Rouge automobile factory to take raw material in and send finished automobiles out, he knew the process would involve recycling. Long before today's environmental movement, Ford set up recycling centers in his factories. You can do something similar by creating a home or (with your teacher's permission) classroom recycling center. Such an activity can be fun while also slowing the growth of landfills—a good thing for the environment.

You'll Need
- Access to the Internet
- Several large plastic storage containers, such as garbage cans or bins, found at home supply or hardware stores
- Magazines with pictures of household goods
- Scissors
- Glue
- Colored markers
- Several plastic garbage bags

1. Find the recycling center nearest you by visiting Earth911 online at http://search.earth911.com. Find out what items your community's recycling center will accept.

2. Decide how you must separate items for drop-off at the recycling center. This will determine how many containers you will require. If, for example, your recycling center wants you to separate (1) plastic, (2) cardboard, (3) paper, (4) glass, and (5) cans, you will need five storage containers.

3. Choose a location for your home or school recycling center, such as your garage, basement, or a corner of your classroom.

4. Label each container to identify the items to be placed in the bin. You can search magazines for pictures of such items, then cut the pictures out and glue them to the containers. Or use colored markers to write the names of the items on the containers. Use your imagination.

5. Arrange the containers in the designated recycling area and line each with a trash bag to make removal of the recyclable items easier.

6. Rinse out bottles and cans before recycling them. Flatten drink cans and cardboard boxes in order to save space in your bins.

7. Once your bins are full, take your recyclables to your community's recycling center. From now on, make recycling an ongoing family or classroom activity.

FROM 1912 TO THE LATE 1930S, the Ford Motor Company issued employee badges that were often works of art and craftsmanship in themselves. Some were made of stainless steel or brass. They were the pride of the wearer, and have become collectible items today. Often a badge showed an image of the plant where the employee worked, or the model car being manufactured at the time. The letters and numbers on a badge identified a particular building, department, and employee.

In this activity, you design a badge reflecting your membership in a group, team, club, or other organization, such as swim team, chorus, chess club, Ms. Sweeny's fifth-grade class, the Anderson family—any group you're proud to be a part of.

You'll Need
- White paper, 8½ inches by 11 inches (21.6 centimeters by 27.9 centimeters)
- Pencil
- Eraser
- Colored pencils, crayons, or markers
- Scissors
- Construction paper, various colors
- Embellishments such as beads, tiny trinkets, bottle caps, broken toy parts, etc.
- Glue

1. Before you begin, spend time thinking about what your badge will look like. Below are some typical Ford badges.

2. Draw the basic shape of your badge: rectangle, triangle, oval, circle, or any shape you want. It might be easier to draw your badge two to four times larger than actual size. If you wish, you can photocopy (and enlarge) a shape at right.

3. Within the outline for your badge, draw the design you wish to create. It is best to draw with a pencil so you can alter your design until you're happy with it.

4. Use colored pencils, crayons, markers, or cut-out shapes from construction paper to add color. If you like, use embellishments to decorate your badge.

5. Your teacher may want you to stand up in class and present your badge. Describe what the design means to you.

crowds descended on showrooms in Dallas, New Orleans, Cleveland, Kansas City, and Denver.

In the first 36 hours that the Model A was on exhibit, it is estimated that 10 million people viewed the new Ford. By the end of its first week of presentation, 25 million people, almost 20 percent of the nation's population, had examined the Model A. Overseas, police were called in to break up fights in Berlin. In Madrid, 150,000 people pushed and shoved to take in the new technological marvel from the United States.

Many chose to see the new Ford as a baby Lincoln. The Model A did not, however, have a Lincoln price tag. The basic **roadster** was advertised at $350. The more spacious **sedan** cost $570. Both prices were no higher than the last Model Ts.

As with the early Model Ts, Henry Ford's biggest problem now would be in satisfying demand. It would take a full year to get up to speed with delivery. But by the end of 1928, the Ford Motor Company was producing 6,400 Model As a day, with 788,572 having been sold for the entire year. Henry Ford, with his new Rouge River factory humming, had done it. No one could question his brilliance as an automaker.

Henry Ford and Edsel Ford with a 1928 Model A at the Ford Industrial Exposition in New York City.
From the Collections of the Henry Ford (P.O.4083)

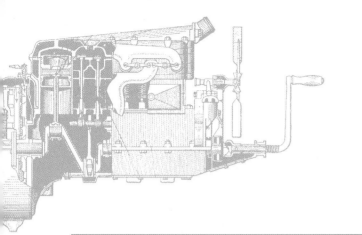

CELEBRATING AMERICA'S RURAL ROOTS

Henry Ford's development of the moving assembly line and its result-ing mass production forever changed the way goods are produced and consumed. Ford's technological achievements would aid in creating the beginnings of an American middle class.

Yet Henry Ford was deeply concerned with what he had helped establish. In an attempt to offset the modern and the industrial (much of which he saw as disturbing), Ford grabbed on to yesterday—in a big way. In time, he would become one of America's most celebrated antiquarians (collector of goods from the past).

After more than a decade of effort, Henry Ford, through his army of searchers, accumulated every example of lamp made in the United States. He owned every kind of doll manufactured since the Revolutionary War. Ford had every known type of harvester. He had a sample of every American smoking pipe, clock, mattress, spinning wheel, chair, candlestick, whiskey jug, birdcage, puzzle, pipe organ, and shoe. By 1927, Ford was well on his way to creating his own private **Smithsonian Institution**, to rival the nation's national museum.

The beginning of Henry Ford's desire to create a "living history," one for people to see and touch, a history not of books but of artifacts, goes back to 1916. On May 5 of that year, the *Chicago Tribune* recorded the industrialist as declaring, "History is more or less bunk. It's tradition. We don't want tradition. We want to live in the present, and the only history that is worth a tinker's damn is the history we make today." Ford went on to say, "History never served me much purpose."

Henry Ford was angry with the way history had been taught to him (and countless other children) in school. His history textbooks focused on the actions of kings, presidents, and generals; this was not Ford's kind of history. What he wanted was a social history, one that focused on ordinary citizens and their daily labors.

Not surprisingly, Ford saw history as a story of progress, particularly in technology. Henry Ford believed that real changes in human life do not come from what governments do. They come from the important inventions we create, such as the steam engine or the telephone. Today, a historian thinking the same way might focus on technology pioneers such as Grace Hopper, Bill Gates, or Steve Jobs.

For Ford, America's story would be "a history of our people as written into things their hands made and used." To that end, Henry Ford built the Edison Institute, in Dearborn, Michigan, its sole purpose educational. "You know, I'm going to prove that history is bunk and give the people an idea of real history," Ford said in 1919. "We are going to show just what actually happened in years gone by."

DANCE FEVER

ONE WAY in which Henry Ford embraced the past was by taking up old-fashioned dancing. Ford, his wife, thousands of schoolchildren, and executives from Highland Park and the Rouge complex would all learn—some willingly, some not—the dances of America's 19th century. In 1926, Henry Ford published a dance manual entitled, *Good Morning: After a Lapse of 25 Years, Old-Fashioned Dancing Is Being Revived by Mr. and Mrs. Henry Ford*. Ford intended to convince his generation that dancing the old Virginia reel, the ripple, the polka, and pop goes the weasel were more fun than the current Charleston.

It all started with Ford hiring dance instructor Benjamin Lovett. Recruited from New England, Lovett would remain in Dearborn for 20 years; he clearly loved his work. Lovett would often arrive to give dance lessons singing "I'm a Yankee Doodle Dandy." A former student of Lovett's dance method commented on how particular and demanding the man's instructions were. "For example, if you were to kick your foot out, you couldn't just kick your foot out. Your toe had to be pointed toward the floor.... It wasn't just any old way, but a certain way."

When Ford said to Lovett, "I have been wondering if we could not start a dancing school for the boys and girls of Dearborn," the dance instructor got the message. Lovett began with a group of just eight students. Soon, more and more kids joined in. Eventually, there would be no less than 22,000 pupils taking old-fashioned dance lessons in Detroit-area schools. In time, coaching spread to 34 colleges, from Michigan to the East Coast.

Executives at the Ford Motor Company were not nearly as enthusiastic. As one observer noted, "For two solid weeks the top brass came to work wilted by nightly polkas and wondered if and when in all hell it would end." Still, they did come (and formally dressed) for their lessons. Ford made it clear there was no choice.

For Henry Ford, it wasn't just the love of traditional dancing that grabbed him; there was the moral issue attached. Ford saw contemporary dances such as the black bottom and the Charles-

ton as shocking. Ford believed people often used these dances as an excuse to engage in inappropriate groping. Old-fashioned dancing, on the other hand, was clean and healthful. Ford's dancers, he insisted, practiced self-discipline and self-respect. Dances such as the waltz built character and class.

Henry Ford and his wife would continue promoting old-fashioned dancing into the early 1940s. It was all part of their reach back to a simpler, rural America.

Benjamin Lovett (far left, holding baton) teaching a dance class in 1944.
From the Collections of the Henry Ford (P.188.71996)

DANCE THE WALTZ

HENRY FORD LOVED TO DANCE. But he hated the newfangled jazz dances of the 1920s. Ford saw them as vulgar and loud. The industrialist preferred traditional old-style dances, such as square dances, contras, the polka, and particularly the waltz.

In this activity, you learn the basic steps for the waltz, a dance that took hold in the United States during the last half of the 19th century.

The waltz is danced to a 1-2-3 beat, in $\frac{3}{4}$ time. When dancing the waltz, you want to try for a graceful, gliding appearance.

Below is a list of websites that will provide additional instruction on how to dance the waltz. For the music, simply go online and search for "waltz dance music." You will find YouTube videos and music you can purchase.

www.dancetv.com/tutorial/waltz
/waltz1.html
www.ballroomdancers.com/dances
/dance_overview.asp?Dance=WAL
www.wikihow.com/Dance-the-Waltz

You'll Need
⚙ You and a partner
⚙ Waltz dance music

1. The waltz is danced in the closed position. The boy places his right hand on the girl's waist and his left hand in her right hand. The girl's left hand is on the boy's right shoulder. Traditionally, a boy leads and a girl follows.

2. Listen to the music and get the 1-2-3 beat. Count the music off as "boom-tick-tick, boom-tick-tick, and lean." The lean is important to facilitate a graceful motion.

3. The basic count (beat) is listed in the chart. The boy's foot pattern is shown in the picture.

4. On the first beat, the boy steps forward with his left foot. The girl mirrors her partner, stepping back with her right foot.

5. On the second beat, the boy steps forward and to the right with his right foot. He should move in an upside-down L shape to get there, while gently leaning into the movement. The girl should move her left foot back and to the left.

6. On the third beat, the boy slides his left foot over to his right foot (close). He will now be standing with his feet together. The girl should mirror the boy's steps, sliding her right foot toward her left foot to close.

7. On the fourth beat, the boy steps back with his right foot. The girl steps forward with her left foot.

8. On the fifth beat, the boy steps back and to the left with his left foot, and the girl steps forward and to the right with her right foot.

9. On the sixth beat, the boy slides his right foot to the left until his two feet are together (close). The girl slides her left foot (close).

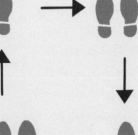

COUNT	BOY'S PART	GIRL'S PART
1	Left foot forward	Right foot back
2	Right foot side	Left foot side
3	Left foot close	Right foot close
4	Right foot back	Left foot forward
5	Left foot side	Right foot side
6	Right foot close	Left foot close

10. Starting again with step 4, the partners repeat the pattern again.

The waltz is a classic dance, as popular today as it ever was. Enjoy!

THE SEARCHERS

To ACQUIRE antiques from which to build a collection of what is today called **Americana**, Ford hired a team of acquisition agents, his "searchers." One group would take New England, approaching the owners of old barns and farm houses. Another combed the western states. A third squad of searchers took the country's middle, the Midwest, with a particular interest in old pieces of farm machinery. What all of Henry Ford's agents had in common was their hunt for everyday objects. Most antique dealers look for rare and valuable items. Ford wanted familiar ones.

Henry Ford would often accompany an agent, taking a hand in the actual purchasing. Upon entering an antique store, Ford would, according to one associate, "walk around and say 'I want this, I want that.' And before he got through, we'd have a carload out of that doggone place with no reference to price at all." In some cases, Ford would simply buy out the store's entire stock.

In May 1926, the *New York Times*, following Ford's every move in his collecting ventures, headlined, OLD PLOWS ADDED TO FORD'S RELICS. The *Times* went on to declare, "A Biddeford, Maine, livery stable keeper has given two plows, one 225 years old, the other 160, to Henry Ford. Exhibited beside one of Mr. Ford's farm tractors and a set of modern 'gang' plows, the ancient farming implements would serve to emphasize the remarkable advance made within the past two centuries in tools used for tilling the soil."

With unlimited funds at the searchers' disposal, thanks to their patron's incredible wealth, old items arriving back in Dearborn multiplied rapidly. Where to put everything became a real problem. A huge replica of Philadelphia's Independence Hall was built to accommodate the acquisitions, though in the end it would house only a small fraction of what was on hand. What Ford had acquired was beginning to look like what one writer called "The worlds' biggest rummage sale."

Indeed, Eunice Fuller Barnard, writing in the *New York Times Magazine*, cataloged but a tiny portion when she declared:

> Down these corridors are ranged in priceless vistas hundreds of old mahogany and maple and burled walnut chairs, highboys, desks, and tables that would make your common collector gnash [grind] his teeth in envy.... Watches, mirrors, music boxes and band instruments, each probably the most complete collection in the world; all sorts of pianos and small organs—virginal spinet, and harpsichord.... Here are the high-wheeled bicycles and sewing machines.... Here are hearses and barber chairs, hobby horses and cradles, early fire engines from New England, the first phonographs and movie cameras, all kinds of vehicles and the earliest automobiles in America.

All of this, Henry Ford would announce in 1929, was to be a gift to the American people.

LEARNING BY DOING

ON OCTOBER 21, 1929, the Henry Ford Museum and Greenfield Village opened up. It would remain a work in progress for decades to come. Indeed, it is not finished today—nor will it ever be.

The Village contains nearly 100 historical structures. Some are re-creations, but many others were painstakingly disassembled at their original locations and their parts carted off to Dearborn, where they were then reassembled.

There are buildings that illustrate aspects of daily life 300 years ago. Some structures are associated with famous figures in America's past, such as the Logan County Courthouse, where Abraham Lincoln argued cases as a young lawyer. A few buildings are reproductions from the early 19th century, created in the Greek Revival style.

There are also buildings associated with Henry Ford's own life, including a replica of the Bagley Avenue shop where Ford built his Quadricycle.

ACTIVITY
EXPLORE "THE HENRY FORD"

THE HENRY FORD is an amazing place. Located in Dearborn, Michigan, the complex consists of the Henry Ford Museum, Greenfield Village, an IMAX theater, the Benson Ford Research Center, and, by way of a tour, the Ford Rouge Factory. The website (www.thehenryford.org) is designed to prepare you for an actual on-site visit. But even if you do not plan such a visit soon, exploring the website is educational and fun in itself. In this activity you build your own online, virtual exhibit as a way to investigate all the site has to offer.

You'll Need
⚙ Computer with Internet access

1. Go to The Henry Ford website at www.thehenry ford.org.

2. Follow these links that will take you to the resources you need to build your exhibit: Resources, Education, Students, Exhibit Builder, Exhibit Builder Help, and finally For Students. (Or you can go directly to http://collections.thehenryford .org/ExhibitHelp.aspx.)

3. Follow the instructions to create your own exhibit. When you are done, share your exhibit with classmates, friends, and family.

The Henry Ford Trade School (Ford Apprentice School) at the Rouge River plant in 1938.
From the Collections of the Henry Ford (P.833.69954)

Ford's childhood home was eventually restored and moved to the Village, placed not far from the re-created homes of other prominent Americans.

In addition to these structures filled with countless artifacts, Greenfield Village had a school. Known as the Ford Trade School, it took in students, some from disadvantaged backgrounds. Students at this school would learn by doing, through field trips, arts and crafts, and a work-study program. At one point, two-thirds of school time was devoted to actual work at Ford Motor Company plants, with pay. By 1927, 4,500 students were enrolled in the trade school, taught by 150 instructors.

Critics ridiculed the Greenfield Village concept from the start, seeing it as nothing more than nostalgia. "In quaint little shops, scattered here and there, hoary [extremely old] handicraft workers ply their trades," one disapproving author noted.

Yet Ford remained untroubled by such criticism. "I have not spent twenty-five years making these collections simply to bring a homesick tear to sentimental eyes," he insisted. "It's serious, not sentimental."

That sentimentality would be put to the test, however, when, on October 21, 1929, Ford's idol, Thomas Edison, arrived for Greenfield Village's most significant, historic dedication.

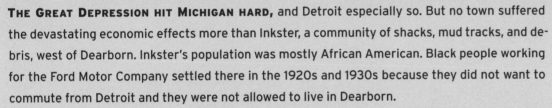

Inkster

THE GREAT DEPRESSION HIT MICHIGAN HARD, and Detroit especially so. But no town suffered the devastating economic effects more than Inkster, a community of shacks, mud tracks, and debris, west of Dearborn. Inkster's population was mostly African American. Black people working for the Ford Motor Company settled there in the 1920s and 1930s because they did not want to commute from Detroit and they were not allowed to live in Dearborn.

So bad was the situation in Inkster, its police force had simply dissolved. The town's electricity was cut off. Garbage pickup disappeared. Most of Inkster's families were in chronic debt. Malnutrition was rampant. Children suffered from rickets (a deficiency disease that affects the young). The town's only bank closed.

In November 1931, Henry Ford decided to do something about the deplorable situation in Inkster. He set up a supermarket that would sell food at wholesale prices. He provided seeds for people to grow their own food. Ford reopened the local school and established a medical clinic. The industrialist purchased sewing machines for the women and organized sewing classes.

Henry Ford paid workers $4 a day to clean up their town. Each worker kept one dollar, with the other three dollars going to fund a revival of community services.

It worked—within a few months the town of Inkster was back on its feet. Many African Americans never forgot what Ford did for them. As one resident later declared, "Without Ford, Inkster would have disappeared."

LIGHT'S GOLDEN JUBILEE

IT WOULD be a celebration like no other, one to champion Henry Ford's view of history. To celebrate the 50th anniversary of the first successful incandescent lightbulb, Ford gathered an impressive list of dignitaries. The 260 people attending included George Eastman (photography), John D. Rockefeller (oil), Will Rogers (humor), Marie Curie (physics), and Orville Wright (flight).

Henry Ford and Thomas A. Edison having a word around 1930.

Library of Congress LC-DIG-det-4a27699

Albert Einstein talked to Edison by telephone from Berlin. President Herbert Hoover was there to offer his congratulations. Dubbed Light's Golden Jubilee, Henry Ford's tribute to the 82-year-old Edison was broadcast to millions of Americans via 140 radio stations.

In Greenfield Village, Ford had reassembled the very same laboratory used by Edison in New Jersey. The industrialist even had a yard full of New Jersey soil transported to the re-created laboratory to increase its authenticity.

When Edison saw what Ford had done, he said, "You got it ninety-nine percent right." What's the 1 percent? Ford wanted to know. "The floor's too clean," Edison replied. Then the great inventor, emotionally overcome, stood and wept. When Edison recovered, he said he could sit right down and start working with his old tools.

To that end, Edison ignited the main event. The next day's *New York Times* headline reported: Edison Re-Creates His Electric Lamp. The article's author, Bruce Rae, went on in near-poetic terms, "Thomas Alva Edison, whose fingers magically woke the world to a new brilliance fifty years ago, stood tonight over the battered work table in the same laboratory in which he made his original experiments and with trembling hands reconstructed his incandescent lamp."

With Henry Ford and Francis Jehl (an original helper 50 years before) standing at his side, Edison had taken two wires from a power source, feeding

The reassembled Menlo Park, New Jersey, laboratory of Thomas Edison, at the Ford Greenfield Village.
Wikimedia Commons

electricity to the lightbulb. It glowed brilliantly. In tribute, millions of Americans turned on lights all across the nation. Edison was so exhausted and overcome with emotion, he fell to a nearby couch and again cried.

It was a glorious occasion, one filled with light and hope for things to come. Edison promised Americans a future in which the setting sun presented "no obstacles" to human activity.

Brighter times, however, would be postponed. On October 29, 1929, just eight days after the Light's Golden Jubilee extravaganza, the stock market crashed. What followed would be 12 years of Great Depression—the worst economic disaster ever to befall the country. The Ford Motor Company, along with all other American car manufacturers, would be sent reeling. Some would never recover.

⚙

Thomas Edison, Henry Ford, and Francis Jehl at the re-created Menlo Park Laboratory in Greenfield Village during Light's Golden Jubilee, in 1929.
From the Collections of the Henry Ford (P.O.922.A)

Finished cars at the end of an assembly line at the Ford Motor Company in Long Beach, California, in 1936.

Library of Congress HAER
CAL,19-LONGB,2-A—91

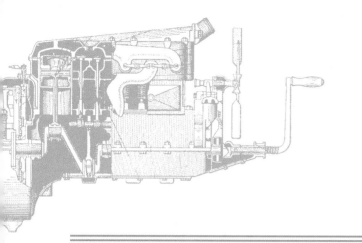

9

TARNISHED HERO

I n the early 1930s, as the country fell deeper and deeper into the worst economic collapse in its history, many laborers were out of work.

The Great Depression of the 1930s was cruel indeed. Many people went hungry; some even starved to death. In Detroit, one out of three working-aged people was without work. In Chicago, it was 40 percent. A whopping 50 percent could not find work in the state of Colorado. New York City was unable to provide employment for 800,000 people who desperately wanted work.

Henry Ford thought he had an answer to the nation's economic ills. According to him, the country needed to focus on three fundamental business principles. As the Depression deepened, Ford declared, "(1) Make or sell the best possible product at the lowest possible price. (2) The best possible product (or service) is one that best fills a real human need. (3) In the course of making or selling, pay the highest possible wages for the shortest possible number of hours."

On July 29, 1931, Henry Ford laid off 75,000 workers and closed 25 of his 36 US assembly plants, as sales of his new car plummeted. Some of the factories that remained open cut operations to four and then three days a week. By 1932, the Ford Motor Company had only six plants in operation. For Ford, sticking to his own business principles was becoming ever harder to do.

In an attempt to reverse the slide in Model A sales, Henry Ford took a bold—and secret—step. In the summer of 1930, Ford placed three of his top engineers in a small, rustic building hidden within Greenfield Village. Ford told one of them, Emil Zoerlein, "What you work on and what you see back there I want you to keep to yourself and not say a word to anybody about it. We are designing a V-8 engine."

What emerged from that building in 1932 and exploded into a massive engineering effort costing more than $300 million was the first low-cost Ford V-8 car. Having eight cylinders instead of the customary four, the new car was far more powerful. The cylinders were placed in a V configuration, as opposed to a straight line, to save engine space. The new car came with a speedometer that could swing its pointer to 80 miles per hour.

"TOO BIG TO BE HUMAN"

THE 1932 Ford V-8 was an engineering marvel. Though it was by no means the first V-8 automobile engine, it was the first *low-cost* V-8. Designing a complex V-8 motor block that could be cast in one piece, and thus inexpensively, was a major challenge. Henry Ford was once again up to the task. And while many engineers worked long hours to make the Ford V-8 a reality, the company's near-70-year-old founder deserves significant credit. When it came to designing and bringing into production a new automotive product, Henry Ford had no equal.

There was great public interest in the car—but less public enthusiasm. Ford's V-8 proved a tough sell. As one would-be customer declared, comparing the new Ford engine to the traditional four-cylinder version, "Twice the cylinders take twice the gas!" Not only gas. The V-8 was also a mighty oil guzzler. Most important, few people could afford the new car even if it sold between $460 and $650. The Depression made the sale of any new car a challenge.

With the country's economy still not having reached bottom, the Ford Motor Company, indeed, all car companies, looked for any way to reduce costs. To that end, once again the speedup took center stage.

The Ford foremen were the driving force in keeping every worker struggling to his or her maximum. One way of increasing employee effort was with the official company yell. It was reported, "Foremen kept a close eye on production numbers, constantly tallied output on an hourly basis, and dashed back to the aisles—up one and down another—shouting 'Let's Go! Let's Go!' And the nearer it gets to the end of the hour the louder and more persistent becomes the yell."

Where, employees at Ford began to wonder, was the Henry Ford of old, the worker's friend? "Driven at an inhuman pace by foremen picked for their brutality, kicked out for any slowing up, shifted to other departments at a lower salary or fired and then rehired at a lower wage, workers scoffed at official company publicity, which blared forth how well Ford treated his employees," wrote Carol Gelderman. Workers worked fewer hours but received less pay. Yet they were required to do the same amount of work. Ford employees wondered what happened to the younger Henry Ford, the one who treated his people fairly and paid them the highest wage in the automotive industry.

With the Great Depression weighing him down, Henry Ford summed up his attitude toward his workers and his company when he declared, "A great business is really too big to be human."

A V-8 engine assembly line at the Ford Rouge River plant, in 1937. From the Collections of the Henry Ford (P.833.68057.105)

THE FORD HUNGER MARCH

Women working in the welding department at the Lincoln Motor Company, Detroit, Michigan, sometime between 1914 and 1918.

Library of Congress LC-USZ62-111143

HENRY FORD had not always felt that there was no room for the humanitarian element in his company. On the contrary, in the early 1920s, after World War I, Ford made a practice of hiring workers that many others in his industry would not.

When it came to employing the disabled, African Americans, women, various ethnic groups, and even ex-criminals, Ford's enlightened policies were decades ahead of their time. "I think that if an industrial institution is to fill its whole role, it ought to be possible for a cross-section of its employees to show about the same proportions as a cross-section of society in general," Ford was proud to state.

In 1919, when World War I ended, the Ford Motor Company employed 9,563 persons with some sort of disability. According to one account, "One had lost both hands; four both legs or feet; four more were totally blind; 123 had lost one hand or arm; 460 had only one good eye; 37 were deaf and dumb; 60 were epileptics; 1,560 had **hernias**." Up until 1919, not a single worker had been let go because of physical disability.

Samuel S. Marquis, who worked closely with Henry Ford for many years, tells the story of a totally blind man sent to work at Ford. The blind man's foreman brought two sighted workers to the employment manager. "Here," he said, "take these men and transfer them to some other department. I don't need them. That blind man you gave me the other day is doing their work and his, too, and they are only in his way. And what's more he keeps singing all the time he's working!"

Ten years later, much at Ford had changed.

On March 7, 1932, several thousand people including hungry, out-of-work men and their families, as well as union organizers, marched on the Ford Rouge River plant. Their objective was to present a formal petition demanding jobs, reduction of the speedup, two daily 15-minute rest periods on the Ford line, and the right to join a union, among other requests. When the marchers approached the Ford plant, 30 to 40 Dearborn police were waiting. They were armed with tear gas and gas bombs.

Immediately, Harry Bennett and his private Ford Service Department appeared, ready to aid the Dearborn police. "From a connection made inside the plant, two high-pressure fire-hoses were run on to the overhead bridge opposite Gate 3," it was reported. "From the vantage point of this overpass, icy streams of water were sprayed into the crowd below."

Within minutes, the situation collapsed into chaos. A submachine gun at the Ford plant gate opened fire on the crowd. Four people were shot dead. Many more were wounded.

No one at the Ford Motor Company would ever be held responsible for those killed and disabled. Harry Bennett, who had been seriously injured by a brick thrown at his head, was given a new Lincoln car by his boss, Henry Ford. The luxury automobile was a reward for his valor (as Ford saw it) in the face of trouble.

LEARN SOME RULES OF THE ROAD

WHEN HENRY FORD experimented with his first automobiles, he did not have a driver's license. Basically, they did not exist. Today, everyone who drives a car needs to be licensed and prove they know the rules of the road. In this activity you begin to learn some of those rules. You are never too young to do so; if you ever ride a bike on the streets, then you, should know many of these rules of the road.

You'll Need
- Notebook paper
- Pencil

As you are riding your bike or being driven around town by an adult, look for the 10 signs below.

Identify the signs by matching each letter to its corresponding numbered name.

a._____   b._____

c._____   d._____

e._____   f._____

g._____   h._____

i._____   j._____

1. Merging Traffic   6. Sharp Turn
2. Lane Ends   7. Winding Road
3. Slippery When Wet   8. T Intersection
4. Yield Ahead   9. Curve
5. Reverse Turn   10. Pedestrian Crossing

Continued...

LEARN SOME RULES OF THE ROAD *Continued*

Answer the following written driver's test questions that are likely to appear on any state driving test:

1. When you drive through a construction zone, you should:

a. Slow down to watch the workers.

b. Decrease your following distance.

c. Pass the construction zone carefully and not "rubberneck."

2. To make a right turn at the corner, you:

a. May not enter the bicycle lane.

b. Should only merge into the bicycle lane if you stop before turning.

c. Must merge into the bicycle lane before turning.

3. If a traffic signal light is not working, you must:

a. Stop, then proceed when safe.

b. Stop before entering the intersection and let all other traffic go first.

c. Slow down or stop, only if necessary.

4. A pedestrian is crossing your lane but there is no marked crosswalk. You should:

a. Make sure the pedestrian sees you, but continue driving.

b. Carefully drive around the pedestrian.

c. Stop and let the pedestrian cross the street.

5. Always use your seat belt:

a. Unless the vehicle was built before 1978.

b. Unless you are in a limousine.

c. When the vehicle is equipped with seat belts.

6. Allow extra space on the road in front of a large truck for:

a. Other drivers when merging onto a freeway.

b. The truck driver to stop the vehicle.

c. Other drivers when they want to slow down.

7. Roads are slippery after it first starts to rain. When the road is slippery you should:

a. Avoid making fast turns and fast stops.

b. Test your tires' traction while going uphill.

c. Decrease the distance you look ahead of your vehicle.

8. Collisions can happen more often when:

a. All vehicles are traveling about the same speed.

b. One lane of traffic is traveling faster than the other lanes.

c. One vehicle is traveling faster or slower than the flow of traffic.

ANSWERS
Warning Signs: a. 3, b. 1, c. 6, d. 2, e. 10, f. 4, g. 9, h. 8, i. 5, j. 7
Test: 1. c, 2. c, 3. a, 4. c, 5. c, 6. b, 7. a, 8. c

THE BATTLE OF THE OVERPASS

IN 1935, the US Congress passed, and President Franklin D. Roosevelt signed into law, the Wagner Act. The bill guaranteed workers the right to form unions, and thus bargain collectively for workers' rights. The act set up the National Labor Relations Board (NLRB) to enforce the law.

Henry Ford was not happy with the Wagner Act; in fact, he was furious. As far back as 1916, the industrialist expressed his dislike (some would say outright hatred) for organized labor when he declared, "Unions mean class war, and I don't believe in war." Ford was offended by the suggestion that a union was needed in his factories. He saw himself as a paternal figure, as a man who would take care of his workers, like a father looks out for his children. "We recognize human beings and their right to a just wage," Ford said. He believed the only labor agreement necessary was one between consenting individuals; between employer and employee.

Henry Ford's opposition to organized labor and the formation and growth of the United Auto Workers (UAW) Union set the stage for confrontation.

In early 1937, the UAW signed collective bargaining agreements with General Motors and Chrysler. Henry Ford's response was swift and steadfast. "We will never recognize the United Auto Workers' Union or any other union. Labor union organizations are the worst thing that ever struck the earth because they take away a man's independence."

Yet, in defense of the act that bears his name, Senator Robert Wagner declared: "It [the Wagner Act] merely provides that employees, if they desire to do so, shall be free to organize for their mutual protection of benefit … it does not force or even counsel any employee to join any union if he prefers to deal directly or individually with his employers."

When it came to dealing with the UAW, which would now target the Ford Motor Company as the last union holdout, Henry Ford did not assign his son Edsel to deal with the situation. The senior Ford felt that Edsel, who favored bargaining with the union, would be too soft. Instead he placed his trusted tough guy, Harry Bennett, in charge.

On May 26, 1937, 60 union men appeared at the Rouge plant to distribute handbills printed with quotes from the Wagner Act. Walter Reuther, a dynamic 30-year-old man who for a time had worked for the Ford Motor Company, led the workers. When the group reached the overpass across Miller Road to Gate 4 of the Rouge, they were met by Bennett's thugs. What resulted became known as the Battle of the Overpass. Reuther and his group were attacked and beaten. "It was really an organized, well-handled beating," a protester remembered. "They had professional guys do the job, and they knew how to do it so that you could not retaliate."

"I didn't fight back," Reuther later declared. "I merely tried to guard my face."

As one-sided as the fight was, Bennett's men made a serious blunder when they chose to attack virtually everyone in sight—including reporters and news photographers covering the scene. With the written word and vivid photographs, the next day's newspapers made it clear who was at fault. *Time* magazine published a devastating account of the brutality that took place.

CLARA CRIES, "ENOUGH"

ON APRIL 1, 1941, Henry Ford's worst fears finally came to pass. The UAW called a strike to shut down the Rouge River plant. As a consequence, under great pressure, the Ford Motor Company agreed to hold an election on unionization. The company leadership firmly believed that, given a chance, its workers would reject unionism. They could not have been more wrong.

The election was held on May 21. Only 3 percent said no to unionization. Henry Ford did not accept the results. He insisted he would close his plants rather than let a union in.

The very next day, however, an amazing, almost unbelievable turnabout took place. Henry Ford quickly agreed to everything the UAW wanted— and a whole lot more. Wages would equal the highest in the industry. Union dues would be withheld from paychecks and turned over to the union by

The Battle of the Overpass confrontation in 1937.
Wikimedia Commons

THE WHEELS ON EARLY MODEL TS could not be removed. If a user had a flat tire, he or she had to jack the car up and repair the tire while it was still mounted to the vehicle. In this activity you simulate Model T tire repair on a bicycle. Even if your bicycle does not have a flat tire, you will benefit from learning the procedure. You may want to ask an adult to help you.

You'll Need
- ⚙ A bicycle with tire and air-filled inner tube
- ⚙ Tire pressure gauge
- ⚙ Three plastic bicycle tire levers
- ⚙ Inner tube patch kit (patches, sandpaper, and vulcanizing [hardening] solution), available at bicycle shops
- ⚙ Bicycle air pump

1. Turn the bicycle upside down to better work on one wheel. Do not take the wheel off the bicycle frame. In this activity you want to simulate what a driver would encounter in fixing a flat on a Model T. Since the Model T driver cannot take the wheel off, you should not either.

2. Use the tire pressure gauge's nimble (tip) to drain air from the wheel's inner tube.

3. Use a tire lever to pry the outer tire bead (the tire's edge that sits on the wheel) from the wheel frame close to where a puncture occurred. (If there is no puncture, pick any place on the wheel to do this.) Place a second tire lever about three inches from the first and do the same. Place a third tire lever about three inches from the second and again do the same.

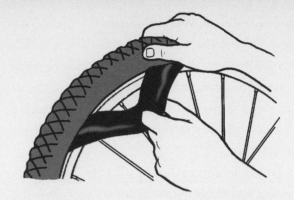

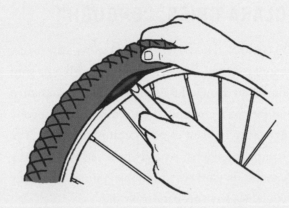

4. Now pull the outer tire bead free from the rim.

5. Pull out a portion of the inner tube where the puncture occurred. If there is no puncture, pull the tube out anyway.

6. Use sandpaper to lightly rough the area to be patched.

7. Apply a thin layer of vulcanizing solution to an area larger than the diameter of the patch. Allow to dry for about two minutes.

8. Press a patch firmly in place. The seal will be made instantly.

9. Place the tube back in the tire and press the outer tire bead back in place. (If necessary, use a tire lever to help.)

10. Pump air into the tire. Use the tire pressure gauge to be sure the tire is inflated to the recommended pressure.

Congratulations! You have learned to fix a flat tire on a bicycle, and you have some idea how Model T drivers repaired punctured tires.

the company. Why, everyone wondered, had this happened? Why had Henry Ford surrendered?

Days later, Ford confessed that his wife had told him that if he did not sign the agreement, "there would be riots and bloodshed, and she had seen enough of that." If Henry persisted in his opposition, Clara added, she would leave him.

"What could I do?" Ford said. "The whole thing was not worth the trouble it would make. I felt her vision and judgment were better than mine." Indeed, Clara Ford, Steven Watts observed, "probably [not for the first time] saved her husband from his own worst instincts."

The election of officers to the Ford Local 600, United Automobile Workers (UAW), in 1942.
Library Congress LC-USW3-016246-C

The Henry Ford Hospital

THE HENRY FORD HOSPITAL, FOUNDED IN 1915, is today one of the leading medical centers in the United States. In the hospital's beginning, Ford had been one of a number of individuals putting up money for its construction. But when only a third of the funds needed were raised, Ford offered to take over the complete financing of the hospital in return for total control. All the other contributors agreed, and Henry Ford had his private hospital, to be built and run as he saw fit.

Ford would design and build his hospital as he did his cars. In the Ford hospital, all rooms would be private or semiprivate and have their own bath. Each one would be the same size.

Ford asked staff doctors for ideas on the perfect size of a hospital room. When they suggested he visit other hospitals throughout the country, the industrialist responded:

I don't care what someone else is doing. What is the right size? How much space do you need? Take the room as your unit. I will give you a carpenter and some wallboard. You know what has to be in each room. You put up a room and try it out, and then keep building rooms until you have exactly the right arrangement of room and bath. When we have the room, then we will make an open model of a floor. Just as soon as we have the unit and the groups of units right, all we have to do is duplicate them and we can have as big a hospital as we want.

As with everything he did, Henry Ford had his own way of doing things.

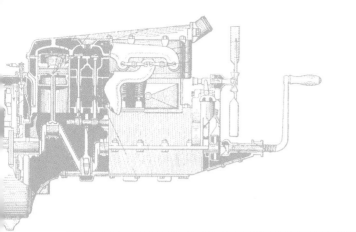

10

RELUCTANT WARRIOR

As the United States headed toward war in the 1940s, Henry Ford, until now a reluctant warrior, devoted his last years and his company's considerable resources and expertise to the war effort. In particular, the Ford Motor Company would mass-produce Liberator bombers.

When it came to flying, though, Henry Ford was no aviator. Yet the automaker met and befriended perhaps the most famous pilot of the 20th century—Charles Lindbergh. When the 25-year-old daredevil flew solo across the Atlantic in 1927, he became an instant international celebrity. Ford, latching on to that fame, twice took to the skies with Lindbergh.

The first takeoff occurred when Lindbergh, visiting Detroit in August 1927, brought Ford up in the *Spirit of St. Louis*, the very airplane that had made the airman famous. "He had to sit bent over, on the arm of my pilot seat," Lindberg later recalled. "But he seemed to enjoy the flight very much." The two flew around above Dearborn for five to ten minutes. Then Ford, casting nervousness aside, allowed Lindbergh to launch him sky-ward once more. This time Ford flew as a copilot in his own recently built, three-engine Ford Tri-Motor, with its 70-foot wingspan.

Henry Ford's interest in aviation began in 1908, the year the first Model T rolled off his assembly line. One of Ford's employees, Charles Van Auken, using Ford Motor Company facilities, built a flying machine, powered by a Model T engine, of course. The airplane, made of wood, metal tubing, and fabric, got into the air but soon after crashed into a tree. Ford said no to any further airplane building, feeling flying was too dangerous.

However, the industrialist would later change his mind. In 1922 he hired an aircraft designer, William Stout, to build what was called the Maiden Detroit, an all-metal airplane with a specially built Ford Liberty motor. Though not much of a success, the Maiden Detroit eventually led to development of a truly pioneering aircraft—the Ford Tri-Motor.

When finally built in 1925, Ford Tri-Motors were used to deliver the US mail across the country. To help pilots find their way, Ford dealers were asked to paint the names of their towns on the roofs of their dealerships. As a Ford executive said, "If every Ford dealer does this in the 10,000 villages, towns, and cities where you represent us, we shall have placed a network of sign boards throughout the United States for the use of air pilots, and we, as well as every air pilot, will appreciate this action on your part."

Charles Lindbergh (in hat) and his airplane, the *Spirit of St. Louis*, in 1927 or 1928.
Library of Congress LC-DIG-hec-34672

The Ford Tri-Motor was a good commercial airplane, with many firsts to its credit. The airplane had an all-metal frame, was outfitted with radio equipment, and its windows were made of safety glass. The aircraft used wheels instead of tail skids. And it was powered by three engines. The Ford Tri-Motor would be affectionately referred to as the Tin Goose.

The Ford Tri-Motors ceased production in 1933. Yet the experience the Ford Motor Company gained in designing and building the airplane prepared them for a much greater aviation project to come 10 years later, during World War II.

THE B-24 LIBERATOR

INITIALLY, HENRY Ford was as opposed to his country entering World War II as he had been to America's involvement in the Great War (now referred to as World War I). A lifelong pacifist, Ford saw war as incredibly wasteful in human lives and the destruction of property. War destroyed; Henry Ford wanted to build.

But when the United States was attacked by the Japanese at Pearl Harbor on December 7, 1941, Ford instantly rose to the occasion as a premier defense contractor. "We are in it now, and the important thing is to finish it quickly, so that we can return to more useful, more serious matters," Ford, the reluctant warrior, declared. "We've got to win this war, so they [the children] can grow up in a free world."

The Grand Cross of the Order of the German Eagle

ON JULY 30, 1938, ON HENRY FORD'S 75TH BIRTHDAY, he was honored by the German government of Adolf Hitler. The German Embassy had contacted an aide to Ford, asking if the industrialist would accept the Grand Cross of the Order of the German Eagle. Such an award was the highest honor any non-German could receive. Ford told his aide, "You tell them that I'll accept anything the German people offer me."

The ceremony was held in Ford's Dearborn office. The medal itself was presented by the German consul. According to the *Detroit News*, the medal came with "a congratulatory message from the Führer Adolf Hitler to Ford on his 75th birthday and citing him as a pioneer in making automobiles available to the masses."

Henry Ford considered Germany to be clean, thrifty, and technologically advanced. It was because of his admiration for such qualities, Ford made clear, that he accepted the award.

Nonetheless, at the time the German government was beginning its campaign against Jews, and Ford's acceptance of the award troubled many Americans, in and out of government. Yet Ford refused to give back the award. Not even the president of the United States could convince Ford to return the medal. No one told Henry Ford what to do.

Regardless of the attention he received from the German government, Henry Ford went on to contribute mightily to the US war effort with his B-24 Bombers and other necessary war weaponry. Once the United States found itself at war, there was no doubt that Henry Ford would do all he could to assure victory.

Though the Ford Motor Company would turn out thousands of cargo trucks, propellers, artillery, light tanks, aircraft engines, and gliders for the war effort, its biggest contribution would be in producing 9,000 four-engine, B-24 Liberator bombers. At one point, the Ford Motor Company assembled a bomber an hour. Initially, Ford had

A B-24 Liberator, built by the Ford Motor Company, on a bombing mission in Europe, in 1944.

Wikimedia Commons

300 miles per hour. Referred to as an ugly duckling because of its stubby fuselage, the airplane could travel 3,000 miles without refueling. It carried up to four tons of bombs.

To build the B-24, Ford constructed the largest bomber factory to operate under one roof. Known as Willow Run because it was located 20 miles west of Dearborn along a small stream of the same name, the plant was a mile long and a quarter of a mile wide. The factory itself sat on 80 acres, with another 100 acres set aside for hangars. There were seven concrete runways, each more than a mile long. Built at government expense for $65 million, Willow Run employed almost 70,000 workers.

With Willow Run, Henry Ford committed everything he had to the war effort. "Two years ago he was an earnest pacifist," *Time* magazine reported in 1942. "Today, like the rest of the industry, he is not only working for war but for war alone.... Henry Ford and his empire have converted themselves to war."

The aging industrialist, however, had little direct involvement with Willow Run. Authority for its operations was given to a key lieutenant, Charles Sorensen, with considerable control also going to Edsel Ford.

Willow Run not only gave employment to tens of thousands of workers, its very existence was a huge boom to the national economy. A reporter, visiting the plant in late 1942, declared, "Willow

promised a thousand airplanes a day—a ridiculous boast.

The B-24 was designed by Consolidated Aircraft of San Diego. With 101,650 parts, the bomber was one of the more complicated aircraft of the war. It had a wingspan of 110 feet and a top speed of

Run is tomorrow's plant built today—for which we have the war to thank. It is, horizontally, what the Empire State Building is vertically, to American industry and architecture.... Willow Run has to be seen to be believed."

DEATH OF A SON

IN JANUARY 1942, Edsel Ford entered the Ford Hospital in Detroit. The operation he endured took out half his stomach. When the president of the Ford Motor Company reentered the hospital 11 months later, his doctors told him what he already knew. Edsel had an ongoing case of **undulant fever**. The disease was a stomach infection that left the sufferer with rising and falling fevers, sweats, uneasiness, weakness, loss of appetite, headache, and muscle pain. Today, undulant fever can be effectively treated with antibiotics. In Edsel's time, no such cure was available.

But undulant fever was only one of Edsel's medical problems and not the most serious. What his doctors did not tell Edsel was that he had stomach cancer, though they knew of it back in January, when they opened him up. What's more, the cancer had spread, soon to enter the liver. Edsel Ford was dying.

Edsel could put on a good face, a calm outward appearance. "I never saw him enthused or laugh about anything or anyone," an associate once observed. But Edsel had many moments of joy in his

SEEING A PICTURE of a Model T Ford is great. Seeing a Model T in a museum or on the road is even better. Best of all, however, is actually taking a ride in a restored Model T. There are two main Model T organizations in the United States. Their names and websites are listed below. By contacting either organization you will find the Model T club nearest you. Every local club has members eager to share their love of the Model T. By approaching your contact in an enthusiastic way, you will soon be taking a ride in an actual Tin Lizzie.

Model T Ford Club of America: www.mtfca .com/clubpages/chapters.htm

The Model T Ford Club International, Inc.: http://1909ford.readyhosting.com/tlist .html

You'll Need
- You and an adult
- Access to the Internet
- A notebook and pen
- A camera

1. Contact one of the two Model T Ford organizations listed above to obtain the address of a club nearest you.

2. Explain what you would like to do. If the contact is agreeable to your request, make arrangements to visit him or her.

3. Before arriving, make a list of 10 to 12 questions for your host. For example, how is a Model T automobile started? How is it driven? What are some of the features that made the Model T so popular?

4. When you meet your host, shake hands and introduce the adults with you. Ask your host to give you a "walk around" of the Model T. Take notes on what is said. Remember, the car is not your property. Be respectful and do not touch any part of the car without permission. Ask your host before taking any pictures.

5. Enjoy the ride! When it's complete, thank your host for his or her time. When you get home, send your host a handwritten thank-you note.

When you were taking the Model T ride, did you notice the reactions of other people on the road? Does it seem that everyone who sees the Model T stops to stare? Why do you think that is?

life. He enjoyed a loving home life with his wife and four children. Edsel's work in the art world, particularly his support of the Diego Rivera murals at the Detroit Institute of the Arts, gave him a great satisfaction.

Henry Ford and Clara Bryant Ford at Edsel Ford's funeral on May 26, 1943.

From the Collections of the Henry Ford (P.833.77996.10)

On May 26, 1943, Edsel Ford died at his home, surrounded by his wife, Eleanor, and three of his four children. He was 49 years old.

Henry Ford's reaction to his son's passing swung between irritation with Edsel's lifestyle and his doctors who could do little for him. His sadness would never go away. "I just can't get over it," Henry Ford told an associate. "I've got a lump right here in my throat. Clara sits down and cries and gets over it, feels a little better. I just cannot do it. I have a lump here and there's nothing I can do about it."

According to many observers, Edsel Ford was never able to challenge the role his father laid out for him. "He had been born to the cough of one of his father's engines," authors Peter Collier and David Horowitz wrote. "As a baby he had been taken for a ride in his father's first car. As a teenager he had worked with his father in the Ford plant. As a young adult he had been made president of the company so that his father could pursue his scheme for total control. As a man he had kept a steadying hand on the company while his father lurched from one scheme to another."

That steady hand would be missed in a country that, in 1943, was still very much at war.

FIGUREHEAD

AT THE time of his son's death in 1943, Henry Ford, soon to turn 80, was in failing health himself.

In 1932, at nearly 70, Ford had undergone surgery for a rare type of hernia, as well as an **appendectomy**. Six years later, the industrialist had a **stroke**, the first of four he would suffer. In 1938, Ford had a second stroke and in 1941 a third one that, according to one writer, "left him with an unclear mind for substantial periods." Charles Sorensen went further, when he said of Ford, "He became a querulous [argumentative], suspicious old man who saw conspiracies everywhere and struggled with a fading memory."

Even with his obvious physical and mental decline, Henry Ford, just a day after Edsel's death, made it clear to the Ford Motor Company's directors that he intended to take over as president again. On June 1, 1943, the board reluctantly agreed to give him the power to run the company once more.

In early 1945, Ford suffered yet another stroke. By May, it was said, "Mr. Ford did know and recognize his immediate family, but probably not many others beyond the family.... Mr. Ford was doing no reasoning." Ford was characterized as "a pleasant vegetable."

On September 21, 1945, at the pleading of his wife, Henry Ford, now a mere **figurehead**, resigned from the Ford Motor Company presidency. His grandson, Henry Ford II, only 25 years old, took over from his grandfather. One of young Henry's first acts was to fire Harry Bennett.

In early April 1947, the weather in Dearborn had turned foul. The rains were so heavy they

A montage showing Henry Ford, Edsel Ford, and the Ford Mack Avenue and Rouge River plants, in 1934.
From the Collections of the Henry Ford (P.833.61115)

knocked out power at the Ford home, known as Fair Lane. The house was now heated by fireplaces and lit only by candles and oil lamps.

Henry Ford retired early for the evening. He had a coughing fit before he went to bed.

A couple of hours later, Ford awoke coughing again and complaining of a headache. His breathing was heavy. A doctor was sent for.

Clara took her husband's head in her hand to comfort him, while giving him sips of water. About

CREATE A GLOSSARY WORD SEARCH

ONE OF THE BEST WAYS to familiarize yourself with words in the glossary is to create a glossary word search.

You'll Need

⚙ Graph paper
⚙ Ruler
⚙ Pencil with an eraser
⚙ Copy of the glossary
⚙ Highlighter pen

1. Using your ruler, draw a square at least 4 inches by 4 inches (10 centimeters by 10 centimeters) on your graph paper. The larger the square, the larger the puzzle, and the more words you will use.

2. Looking at the glossary on page 110, choose words that you will put inside your word search. As you write the word, use uppercase letters, one per square. You can write the words across, up, down, backward, and diagonally. Chose as many words as you like.

3. To the side of your square, keep a list of the words you are using so that players know what to look for.

4. After you have written in all the words you want to use, fill in the blank squares with letters. Wherever possible, use short letter combinations that are part of some of the words you used.

5. Players can identify a word they find with a highlighter pen.

When a player identifies a word, quiz him or her on the meaning. Check the answers by reading the glossary definitions.

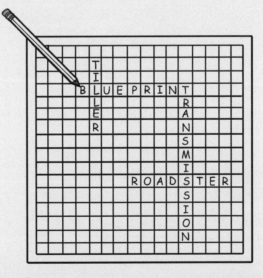

20 minutes before the doctor arrived, Henry Ford took his last breath. The doctor would later speculate that Ford broke a blood vessel in his brain as a result of severe coughing. As Vincent Curcio commented, "Ironically, Henry Ford left the world by candlelight and a wood fire, the same way he came into it 83 years before."

THE HENRY FORD LEGACY

HENRY FORD was a man of monumental contradictions. He put Americans on wheels with the design and production of the Model T. He revolutionized industry with the moving assembly line. Ford believed that his workers deserved a share of company profits, and he gave them a revolutionary profit sharing plan with his $5-a-day wage. Henry Ford founded schools, hospitals, an orphanage, and a museum. He hired the disabled when most others considered them unemployable. While at one time Ford was the richest man in the world, he ultimately gave away at least a third of his income.

Yet Henry Ford had his flaws—as does any human being. The same man that gave workers a huge boost in pay lateor harassed those workers with a private police force. Ford lashed out at Jews, banks, and Wall Street. He wound up firing most of his colleagues, some of whom had been with him from the Ford Motor Company's founding in 1903. While Ford could be enormously innovative, he stubbornly stayed with the outdated Model T way beyond its time. Even though Henry Ford thought that what he was doing with Edsel was best, his treatment of his only son remains questionable.

Henry Ford, in the end, not only gave birth to a modern America, he *was* modern America. For a man who once declared, "History is more or less bunk," Ford has earned a permanent place in it. As the humorist Will Rogers famously announced, "It will take a hundred years to tell if he helped us or hurt us, but he certainly didn't leave us where he found us."

Henry Ford, always the machinist, always the mechanic, in 1933.
Wikimedia Commons

GLOSSARY

Americana Artifacts and objects relating to the folklore and cultural heritage of the United States

anarchist A person who seeks to overthrow the government by violent means

anti-Semitic Hostility toward Jewish people

appendectomy The surgical removal of the appendix (an organ near the stomach), usually performed as an emergency procedure in a hospital

automobile A motor vehicle with four wheels; usually propelled by an internal combustion engine

axle A solid metal shaft to which the wheels of a vehicle are attached

blueprint A drawing showing the manufacture or assembly of mechanical parts

carburetor A device that mixes fuel and air to suit the needs of an engine

coupe A car with two doors as opposed to one with four doors

creditor One who has lent money and to whom the loan must be repaid

custom-built When referring to a car, one built specifically to someone's specifications, as opposed to a mass-produced car

cutter A lightweight, open horse-drawn sleigh, introduced in the United States in about 1800

dividend A share of profits paid to a stockholder

figurehead A person who has a high title in an organization, but doesn't hold real power

flywheel A tool that stores rotational energy by resisting the changes in rotational speed

flywheel magneto The combination of a *flywheel* and *magneto* to generate electricity for the ignition in an internal combustion engine

ghostwriter A person who writes a book or article, but the authorship credit is given to someone else

hernia A rupture of an internal organ through the skin

horseless carriage An early term for an automobile, as it replaced the horse-drawn carriage

horsepower A standard measurement of how much power a car, truck, etc., has in terms of the pulling power of horses. If a vehicle is rated at 40 horsepower, it has the pulling power of 40 horses

idealist A person who has high ideals that are often unfilled for practical reasons

incandescent lamp A bulb that produces light from an electrically heated filament enclosed in a transparent globe from which air has been removed

internal combustion engine (ICE) An engine that works on power released by vaporized fuel and air burning inside the engine itself

libel Saying or writing something about someone that leaves an unfavorable impression

magneto A small electric generator used to provide high-voltage pulses in the ignition systems of an automobile

mediation An attempt to reconcile differences

mock-up With regard to an automobile, a full-scale model, often molded in clay and wood

mold A frame around an object to be constructed

pacifist A person strongly opposed to war

orthographic projection A multiview drawing used as a guide to manufacture or assemble mechanical parts.

parasite A person who lives off the hospitality of others

pattern A design used for duplicating a product

plaintiff A person who brings legal action against someone or some organization in a court of law

planetary transmission A set of gears in a transmission featuring a central gear called a sun gear, surrounded by two or more smaller planetary gears that mesh with a ring gear

preparedness A military buildup in preparation for war

prototype The first-of-a-kind model of something that, if it works, will be used as a pattern for full production of a product

Quadricycle The name given by Henry Ford to his first four-wheel, gas-powered vehicle, developed in 1896

roadster An open two seated car with emphasis on sporting appearance or character

runabout A small, inexpensive, open car popular at the beginning of the 20th century. Most runabouts had just a single row of seats, providing seating for two passengers. In the vintage vehicle era, nearly half of all car models, and the majority of cars produced, were classified as runabouts

running board A footboard extending along the side of early automobiles

schematic A diagram of a structured framework or plan

sedan An enclosed automobile for four or more people, having two or four doors

shock absorber A device located near each wheel to cut down the vertical bouncing of the passenger compartment

Smithsonian Institution The national museum in Washington, DC, housing artifacts representing the technical achievements of the nation

soup to nuts To include everything; from beginning to end

speedup When an employer, usually in a factory, requires assembly workers to do ever more work in a fixed time period, without any additional pay

stock Money invested in a corporation

stockholder A person who is a part owner of a company by holding *stock* in that company

stroke A condition resulting from a blood clot to a person's brain

tiller A lever used to steer an early automobile. Quickly replaced by a steering wheel

Tin Lizzie An affectionate name for the Model T Ford

touring car An open car seating four or more, popular in the early 20th century, before closed bodies became less expensive in the 1920s

transmission An assembly of gears that mesh in varying arrangements. The transmission enables the vehicle to move forward or backward to meet a variety of driving situations

undulant fever An illness resulting in weakness, headaches, chills, and weight loss as a result of contact with infected domestic animals

vanadium steel A strong, lightweight metal used extensively by Ford in the building of the Model T

vertical integration An enterprise that has acquired all it needs to manufacture a product, without relying on outside sources

PLACES TO VISIT, IN PERSON OR ONLINE

Built in the U.S.A.: Car Factories You Can Tour

www.automobilemag.com/features/news/built-in
-the-u-s-a-car-factories-you-can-tour-152835

If you have some extra time on your next summer vacation, a tour of an automobile factory may be just the thing. At the many plants listed on this site, employees will lead visitors on guided tours.

Edison & Ford Winter Estates

www.edisonfordwinterestates.org

Visitors to the Florida estate can wander over 20 acres of historical buildings, gardens, and the Edison Botanic Research Laboratory. Hundreds of inventions, artifacts, and special exhibits are on display.

The First Car—a History of the Automobile

www.history.com/topics/automobiles/videos

This History Channel site provides a detailed look at the early automobile industry, with an emphasis on Henry Ford's contributions. Numerous videos, some with original footage and reenactments, are available.

Ford Homes in Michigan Open to the Public: Fair Lane and Edsel/Eleanor House

www.fordhouse.org

The visiting experience to these Ford homes is both inspirational and educational, with connections to art, design, history, and the environment.

Ford River Rouge Plant: The Story of a Triumph of an Idea

www.youtube.com/watch?v=TcXfkOop6JA

A 1939 film showing how the Rouge Plant operated in its heyday.

The Henry Ford/Greenfield Village/Ford Factory

www.thehenryford.org

An amazing museum with 18 interactive kiosks (booths), a drive-in theater, events, such as a weekly celebration of American ingenuity, and a tour that puts you in the center of sheer "manufacturing might."

History of Electric Vehicles—Early Years

http://inventors.about.com/od/estartinventions/a/History-Of-Electric-Vehicles.htm

This is a good site to get information on early manufacturers' attempts to build viable electric vehicles. It is useful for researching and writing short school reports on the subject.

Inside the World of Youth Racing

www.caranddriver.com/features/inside-the-world-of-youth-racing-feature

This is a site on the world of Quarter-Midget auto racing for kids, ages five and up. Larger than one-quarter the size of a regular midget racecar, but competing at speeds that are about one-quarter as fast, on a track that is one-quarter as long, this site is an introduction to the world of auto racing.

Model T Ford Club of America

www.mtfca.com/index.htm

Not only does this site connect you with any Model T club in America, it provides a wealth of information on the car itself. If you click on "Encyclopedia," and then pick a date (from 1909 to 1927), you will be presented with detailed information about the Model T of that year. Pictures are also included.

NOTES

Introduction

"If there were no Fords" Watts, *The People's Tycoon*, 126.

"I will build a motorcar" Collier and Horowitz, *The Fords*, 52.

Chapter 1: Farm Boy Mechanic

"I have followed many a weary mile" Ford, *My Life and Work*, 14.

"of medium height, with a muscular strength" Collier and Horowitz, *The Fords*, 15.

"The first thing I remember in my life" Nevins and Hill, *Ford: The Times, the Man, the Company*, 42.

"You must earn the right to play" Collier and Horowitz, *The Fords*, 20.

"Life will give you many unpleasant tasks" Collier and Horowitz, *The Fords*, 20.

"She was that rarest type" Collier and Horowitz, *The Fords*, 20.

"Don't put that back" Watts, *The People's Tycoon*, 466.

"Don't let Henry see them!" Nevins and Hill, *Ford: The Times, the Man, the Company*, 48.

"Henry once bored two small holes" Watts, *The People's Tycoon*, 7.

"Machines are to a mechanic" Curcio, *Henry Ford*, 7.

"Farmers set off for their fields" Watts, *The People's Tycoon*, 6.

"I thought a great wrong" Lacey, *Ford: The Men and the Machine*, 11–12.

"My father was sympathetic and understanding" Nevins and Hill, *Ford: The Times, the Man, the Company*, 73.

"Henry quickly solved a problem" Collier and Horowitz, *The Fords*, 24.

"He's different" Collier and Horowitz, *The Fords*, 26.

Chapter 2: The Ford Motor Company

"On the second attempt" Brinkley, *Wheels for the World*, 19.

"In his determination to build the vehicle" Watts, *The People's Tycoon*, 40.

"While the automobile is European" Rae, *The American Automobile*, 1.

"Genius is one percent" Brinkley, *Wheels for the World*, 24.

"This young fellow who has made" Collier and Horowitz, *The Fords*, 34.

"Young man, you have the right idea" Curcio, *Henry Ford*, 30.

"Well, you won't be seeing much of me" Collier and Horowitz, *The Fords*, 34.

"No man up until that time" Watts, *The People's Tycoon*, 42.

"I had to choose between my job" Ford, *My Life and Work*, 20.

"Henry never put much time in the shop" Watts, *The People's Tycoon*, 55.

"When the shop where Ford and Wills worked" Brinkley, *Wheels for the World*, 37.

"Boy, I'll never do that again" Collier and Horowitz, *The Fords*, 41.

"I cannot quite describe the sensation" Brinkley, *Wheels for the World*, 44.

"Well, this chariot may kill me" Watts, *The People's Tycoon*, 78.

"keep it simple and light" Brooke, *Ford Model T*, 38.

"That put Model B on the map" Brooke, *Ford Model T*, 42.

Chapter 3: Tin Lizzie

"In 1905 I [Henry Ford] was at a motor race" Ford, *My Life and Work*, 38.

"the car that put the world" Brooke, *Ford Model T*, 55.

"For seven days" Nevins and Hill, *Ford: The Times, the Man, the Company*, 405.

"Mr. Ford's theory that a lightweight car" Nevins and Hill, *Ford: The Times, the Man, the Company*, 406.

"Ford—Winner of the Ocean to Ocean Contest" Watts, *The People's Tycoon*, 125.

"The first step forward in assembly came" Ford, *My Life and Work*, 46.

"He does as nearly as possible" Ford, *My Life and Work*, 47.

"One man is now able to do" Ford, *My Life and Work*, 47.

"Employees saw themselves as robot laborers" Collier and Horowitz, *The Fords*, 65.

"The chain system you have is a *slave driver*" Lacey, *Ford*, 138.

"So great was the alienation" Collier and Horowitz, *The Fords*, 65.

"Mr. Ford pay me two-fifty" Brinkley, *Wheels for the World*, 169.

"Workers in the garb of their native" Curcio, *Henry Ford*, 83.

Chapter 4: Peace, War, and Politics

"Any corporation is organized" Sears, *The Automobile in America*, 159.

"I don't believe in preparedness" Gelderman, *Henry Ford*, 92.

"Well boys, we've got a ship" Gelderman, *Henry Ford*, 100–101.

"Now You Stop!" Watts, *The People's Tycoon*, 232.

"Deserves respect, not ridicule" Watts, *The People's Tycoon*, 240.

"I do not regret the attempt" Ford, *My Life and Work*, 144.

"In the event of a declaration of war" Curcio, *Henry Ford*, 97.

"If militarism can be crushed only with militarism" Curcio, *Henry Ford*, 97.

"Each boat made a shakedown cruise" Brinkley, *Wheels for the World*, 216.

"Mr. Ford" Lacey, *Ford*, 169.

"If the people of Michigan choose" Watts, *The People's Tycoon*, 243.

"What do you want to do that for?" Lacey, *Ford*, 170.

"I have made only one speech in my life" Gelderman, *Henry Ford*, 122.

"If they would spend $176,000 to win" Watts, *The People's Tycoon*, 248.

Chapter 5: On the Dark Side

"Ford employees who volunteered to bear arms" Gelderman, *Henry Ford*, 153.

"If Ford allows this rule of his shops to stand" Gelderman, *Henry Ford*, 153–54.

"sought to bring the plaintiff" Watts, *The People's Tycoon*, 266.

"Say, that airplane is flying pretty low" Watts, *The People's Tycoon*, 268.

"Look at that bird there" Watts, *The People's Tycoon*, 368.

"Q: Have there been any revolutions in this country?" Sward, *The Legend of Henry Ford*, 104.

"Do you want to leave it that way" Sward, *The Legend of Henry Ford*, 105.

"Yes, you can leave it that way" Sward, *The Legend of Henry Ford*, 105.

"I don't like to read books" Watts, *The People's Tycoon*, x.

"If you chop your own wood" Ford, *My Life and Work*, 144.

"What was the United States originally?" Sward, *The Legend of Henry Ford*, 105.

"Land, I guess." Sward, *The Legend of Henry Ford*, 105.

"I could find a man in five minutes" Sward, *The Legend of Henry Ford*, 105.

"A few less smart-aleck attorneys" Watts, *The People's Tycoon*, 270–71.

"There is a race" "The International Jew," *Dearborn Independent*, 1.

"Chronicle of the Neglected Truth" Collier and Horowitz, *The Fords*, 103.

"vile, lewd, nasty, erotic, and criminal" Sward, *The Legend of Henry Ford*, 150.

"the 'skunk-cabbage of American Jazz'" Sward, *The Legend of Henry Ford*, 150.

"I would tear down my plants" Baldwin, *Henry Ford and the Jews*, 93.

"The Jew in Character and Business" Ford, *The International Jew*, 3–4.

"An Address to Gentiles" Watts, *The People's Tycoon*, 380.

"urged vigilant citizens to open" Watts, *The People's Tycoon*, 380.

"Jew metal" Watts, *The People's Tycoon*, 384.

"What's wrong, Dr. Franklin?" Curcio, *Henry Ford*, 158.

"I'm going to find out who knocked" Baldwin, *Henry Ford and the Jews*, 222.

"Now you just drop this" Baldwin, *Henry Ford and the Jews*, 222.

"as a plot by Jewish international" Watts, *The People's Tycoon*, 391.

"deeply mortified that his journal" Watts, *The People's Tycoon*, 395.

Chapter 6: Father and Sons

"Henry Ford's greatest achievement" Watts, *The People's Tycoon*, 356.

"I have a million in gold deposited" Collier and Horowitz, *The Fords*, 72.

"He was well-liked by everybody" Watts, *The People's Tycoon*, 359.

"As cars became more complex" Lacey, *Ford*, 268.

"Mrs. Ford, Through Sympathy" *New York Times*, February 6, 1922, 1.

"Ford Pays $8,000,000 Check" *New York Times*, February 12, 1922, 1.

"Father made the most popular car" Collier and Horowitz, *The Fords*, 114.

"I am Mr. Ford's personal man" Gelderman, *Henry Ford*, 298.

"No one could loaf" Gelderman, *Henry Ford*, 319–20.

"You should see my husband come home" Gelderman, *Henry Ford*, 320.

"How did you happen to lose" Brinkley, *Wheels for the World*, 281.

"They checked on men walking around" Gelderman, *Henry Ford*, 321.

"Ford Whisper" Collier and Horowitz, *The Fords*, 161.

"Fordization of the Face" Collier and Horowitz, *The Fords*, 161.

"Millions of Dollars Worth" Gelderman, *Henry Ford*, 188.

"I've never seen a bunch" Watts, *The People's Tycoon*, 261.

Chapter 7: From Soup to Nuts

"What is that over there?" Gelderman, *Henry Ford*, 252.

"Ford took his hands out of his pockets" Gelderman, *Henry Ford*, 252.

"I do not think the Model T" Brooke, *Ford Model T*, 72.

"It [the Model T] was hard-working" Langworth, *The Complete History of the Ford Motor Company*, 66.

"It gets you there and it brings you back" Collier and Horowitz, *The Fords*, 120.

"One sees them all about" Ford, *My Life and Work*, 19.

"After building 15,000,000 automobiles" James C. Young, "Ford's New Car Keeps Motor World Guessing," *New York Times*, June 6, 1927, 1.

"There were too many bolts holding" Langworth, *Complete History*, 71.

"a continuous, nonstop process from" "Ford Rouge Factory Tour: History of the Rouge, Part 1," The Henry Ford website, www.the henryford.org/rouge/historyofrouge.aspx.

"There were ore docks" "Ford Rouge Factory Tour," The Henry Ford website.

"Kahn revolutionized the concept" "Albert Kahn Dies; Famous Architect," *New York Times*, December 9, 1942, 27.

"The public" "Ford Car's Debut Jams Showrooms," *New York Times*, December 3, 1927, 1.

Chapter 8: Celebrating America's Rural Roots

"History is more or less bunk" Fred C. Kelly, "History is Bunk, Says Henry Ford," *New York Times*, October 29, 1921, 66.

"a history of our people as written" "Explore & Learn: Pic of the Month," The Henry Ford website, www.thehenryford.org/exhibits/pic/2004/january.asp.

"You know, I'm going to prove that" Nevins and Hill, *Ford: Expansion and Challenge 1915–1933*, 497.

"For example, if you were to kick" Watts, *The People's Tycoon*, 417–18.

"I have been wondering if we could" Gelderman, *Henry Ford*, 279.

"For two solid weeks the top brass" Watts, *The People's Tycoon*, 418.

"walk around and say" Watts, *The People's Tycoon*, 404.

"A Biddeford, Maine, livery stable keeper" "Old Plows Added to Ford's Relics," *New York Times*, May 16, 1926, 1.

"The worlds' biggest rummage sale" Watts, *The People's Tycoon*, 407.

"Down these corridors are ranged" Eunice Fuller Barnard, "Ford Builds a Unique Museum," *New York Times Magazine*, April 5, 1931, 3.

"In quaint little shops, scattered" Snow, *I Invented the Modern Age*, 326.

"I have not spent twenty-five years" Snow, *I Invented the Modern Age*, 326.

"Without Ford" Curcio, *Henry Ford*, 232.

"You got it ninety-nine percent right" Snow, *I Invented the Modern Age*, 327.

"Thomas Alva Edison, whose fingers magically" Bruce Rae, "Edison Re-Creates His Electric Lamp," *New York Times*, October 22, 1929, 1.

"no obstacles" Freeberg, *The Age of Edison*, 305.

Chapter 9: Tarnished Hero

"(1) Make or sell the best possible product" Ford, *Moving Forward*, 2.

"What you work on and what you see" Langworth, *Complete History*, 84.

"Twice the cylinders take twice" Langworth, *Complete History*, 90.

"Foremen kept a close eye on" Watts, *The People's Tycoon*, 455.

"Driven at an inhuman pace by foremen" Gelderman, *Henry Ford*, 323.

"A great business is really too big" Curcio, *Henry Ford*, 230.

"I think that if an industrial" Curcio, *Henry Ford*, 74.

"One had lost both hands" Nevins and Hill, *Ford: The Times, the Man, the Company*, 562.

"Here," he said, "take these men" Marquis, *Henry Ford: An Interpretation*, 111–12.

"From a connection made inside the" Sward, *The Legend of Henry Ford*, 235.

"Unions mean class war" Watts, *The People's Tycoon*, 458.

"We recognize human beings" Watts, *The People's Tycoon*, 458.

"It [the Wagner Act] merely" Speech of the National Labor Relations Act, Congressional Record, 74th Congress, 1st Session, Volume 9, February 21, 1935, http://web.mit.edu/course

/21/21h.102/www/Primary%20source%20 collections/The%20New%20Deal/Wagner ,%20National%20Labor%20Relations%20 Act.htm.

"We will never recognize the" Gelderman, *Henry Ford*, 328.

"It was really an organized" Gelderman, *Henry Ford*, 330.

"I didn't fight back" Gelderman, *Henry Ford*, 330.

"I don't care what someone else" Gelderman, *Henry Ford*, 199–200.

"there would be riots and bloodshed" Watts, *The People's Tycoon*, 462.

"What could I do?" Sorensen, *My Forty Years with Ford*, 171.

"probably not for the first time" Watts, *The People's Tycoon*, 462.

Chapter 10: Reluctant Warrior

"He had to sit bent over" Brinkley, *Wheels for the World*, 327.

"If every Ford dealer does this" Gelderman, *Henry Ford*, 350–51.

"We are in it now" Watts, *The People's Tycoon*, 508.

"Two years ago he was" "The Battle of Detroit," *Time*, March 23, 1942, 10, 14.

"Willow Run is tomorrow's" Lewis, *The Public Image of Henry Ford*, 361.

"I never saw him" Watts, *The People's Tycoon*, 514.

"He is high-strung, nervous" Watts, *The People's Tycoon*, 514.

"I just can't get over it" Collier and Horowitz, *The Fords*, 191.

"He had been born to the cough" Collier and Horowitz, *The Fords*, 190.

"You tell them that I'll" Watts, *The People's Tycoon*, 397.

"a congratulatory message" David L. Lewis, "Reich Honor Is Bestowed," *Detroit News*, July 31, 1938, 1.

"left him with an unclear mind" Watts, *The People's Tycoon*, 502.

"He became a querulous" Sorensen, *My Forty Years with Ford*, 266.

"Mr. Ford did know and recognize" Watts, *The People's Tycoon*, 525.

"Ironically, Henry Ford" Curcio, *Henry Ford*, 266.

"History is more or less bunk" Fred C. Kelly, "History is Bunk, Says Henry Ford," *New York Times*, October 29, 1921, 66.

"It will take a hundred years" Curcio, *Henry Ford*, 274.

BIBLIOGRAPHY

✿ Denotes sources most suitable for young readers.

Bak, Richard. *Henry and Edsel: The Creation of the Ford Empire.* Hoboken, NJ: John Wiley & Sons, 2003.

Baldwin, Neil. *Henry Ford and the Jews: The Mass Production of Hate.* New York: Public Affairs, 2003.

Brauer, Norman. *There to Breathe the Beauty: The Camping Trips of Henry Ford, Thomas Edison, Harvey Firestone, and John Burroughs.* Dalton, PA: Norma Brauer, 1995.

Brinkley, Douglas. *Wheels for the World: Henry Ford, His Company, and a Century of Progress 1903–2003.* New York: Penguin, 2004.

✿ Brooke, Lindsay. *Ford Model T: The Car that Put the World on Wheels.* Minneapolis: Motorbooks, 2008.

Bryan, Ford R. *Beyond the Model T: The Other Ventures of Henry Ford.* Detroit: Wayne State University Press, 1997.

Cabadas, Joseph P. *River Rouge: Ford's Industrial Colossus.* St. Paul, MN: Motorbooks International, 2004.

Chandler, D. Alfred, Jr. *Giant Enterprise: Ford, General Motors, and the Automobile Industry.* New York: Harcourt, Brace & World, 1964.

✿ Clymer, Floyd. *Those Wonderful Old Automobiles.* New York: Bonanza Books, 1953.

Collier, Peter, and David Horowitz. *The Fords: An American Epic.* New York: Summit, 1987.

Curcio, Vincent. *Henry Ford.* New York: Oxford University Press, 2013.

Ford, Henry. *The International Jew.* San Bernardino, CA: Filiquarian/Qontro, 2007.

Ford, Henry. *Moving Forward.* Garden City, NY: Doubleday, Doran, 1930.

Ford, Henry. *My Life and Work.* San Bernardino, CA: CruGuru, 2008. First published 1922 by Doubleday, Page.

Ford, Henry. *Today and Tomorrow*. Cambridge, MA: Productivity Press, 1988. First published 1926 by Doubleday, Page.

Freeberg, Ernest. *The Age of Edison: Electric Light and the Invention of Modern America*. New York: Penguin, 2014.

Gelderman, Carol. *Henry Ford: The Wayward Capitalist*. New York: Dial Press, 1981.

Ingrassia, Paul. *Engines of Change: A History of the American Dream in Fifteen Cars*. New York: Simon & Schuster, 2012.

Lacey, Robert. *Ford: The Men and the Machine*. New York: Ballantine, 1986.

Langworth, M. Richard. *The Complete History of the Ford Motor Company*. New York: Beekman House, 1987.

Lewis, David. *The Public Image of Henry Ford*. Detroit: Wayne State University Press, 1976.

Lewis, David L. "Reich Honor Is Bestowed." *Detroit News*. July 31, 1938.

Marquis, S. Samuel. *Henry Ford: An Interpretation*. Boston: Little, Brown, 1923.

✿ McCalley, Bruce. *Model T Ford: The Car that Changed the World*. Lola, WI: Krause, 1994.

McCarthy, Pat. *Henry Ford: Building Cars for Everyone*. Berkeley Heights, NJ: Enslow, 2007.

Miller, Ray, and Bruce McCalley. *From Here to Obscurity*. Oceanside, CA: Evergreen, 1971.

✿ Mitchell, Barbara. *We'll Race You, Henry: A Story about Henry Ford*. Minneapolis: Lerner, 1986.

✿ Mitchell, Don. *Driven: A Photobiography of Henry Ford*. Washington, DC: National Geographic, 2010.

Nevins, Allan, and Ernest Hill. *Ford: Decline and Rebirth 1933–1962*. New York: Charles Scribner's Sons, 1963.

Nevins, Allan, and Ernest Hill. *Ford: Expansion and Challenge 1915–1933*. New York: Charles Scribner's Sons, 1954.

Nevins, Allan, and Ernest Hill. *Ford: The Times, the Man, the Company*. New York: Charles Scribner's Sons, 1954.

Newton, James. *Uncommon Friends: Life with Thomas Edison, Henry Ford, Harvey Firestone, Alexis Carrel & Charles Lindbergh*. New York: Harcourt, 1987.

✿ Olson, Sidney. *Young Henry Ford: A Picture History of the First Forty Years*. Detroit: Wayne State University Press, 1963.

Rae, B. John. *The American Automobile: A Brief History*. Chicago: University of Chicago Press, 1965.

Rae, B. John. *American Automobile Manufacturers: A History of the Automobile Industry: The First Forty Years*. New York: Chilton, 1959.

Reuther, G. Victory. *The Brothers Reuther and the Story of the UAW*. Boston: Houghton Mifflin, 1976.

Sclar, Deanna. *Auto Repair for Dummies*. Indianapolis: Wiley, 2009.

Sears, W. Stephen. *The Automobile in America*. New York: American Heritage, 1977.

Smith, Philip Hiller. *Wheels Within Wheels: A Short History of American Motor Car Manufacturing*. New York: Funk & Wagnalls, 1968.

Snow, Richard. *I Invented the Modern Age: The Rise of Henry Ford*. New York: Scribner, 2013.

Sorensen, Charles. *My Forty Years with Ford*. Detroit: Great Lakes Books, 2006.

Sward, Keith. *The Legend of Henry Ford*. New York: Rinehart, 1948.

Time. "The Battle of Detroit." March 23, 1942.

Watts, Steven. *The People's Tycoon: Henry Ford and the American Century*. New York: Vintage, 2005.

✿ Werling, Donn. *Henry Ford: A Hearthside Perspective*. Troy, MI: Society of Automotive Engineers, 2000.

✿ White, E. B. *Farewell to Model T: From Sea to Shining Sea*. New York: Little Bookroom, 2003.

INDEX

Page numbers in *italics* indicate pictures.

V

V-8 engines, 92
Van Auken, Charles, 102
vanadium steel, 24
vertical integration, 74

W

wages, 32, 35, 92
Wagner, Robert, 97
Wagner Act, 96–97
Wall Street, 54
waltz dance (activity), 82

Watts, Stephen, 13
welders, 94
Willow Run factory, 104–105
Wills, C. Harold, 16
Wilson, Woodrow, 41, 44, 55
Winto, Alexander, 17
word search (activity), 108
World War I, 40–42, 44–45
World War II, 103–104

Z

Zoerlein, Emil, 92

ALSO BY RONALD A. REIS

Christopher Columbus and the Age of Exploration for Kids

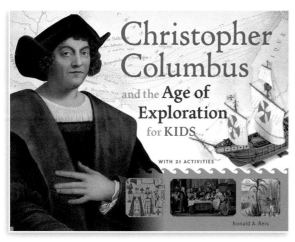

With 21 Activities

ISBN 9781613746745
$16.95 (CAN $18.95)

Christopher Columbus and the Age of Exploration for Kids portrays the "Admiral of the Ocean Seas" neither as hero nor heel but as a flawed and complex man whose significance is undeniably monumental.

"A brilliantly illustrated and well laid out account … I highly recommend it!"

—Luxury Reading

"[*Christopher Columbus and the Age of Exploration for Kids*] marks an important part of our history with fascinating details, fun history, and beautiful art and maps…. This book is great for elementary kids, and little ones will enjoy the pictures and activities."

—Kristen Kemp, Parents.com

The US Congress for Kids

Over 200 Years of Lawmaking, Deal-Breaking, and Compromising, with 21 Activities

ISBN 9781613749777
$16.95 (CAN $19.95)

An interactive guidebook to the history and inner workings of the legislative branch of the US government providing a historical perspective on all that is going on today, *US Congress for Kids* examines the major milestones in congressional history, including the abolition of slavery, extending the vote to African Americans and to women, and investigating misconduct in both government and private institutions.

"It is difficult to not be very cynical when it comes to discussing the US Congress and its members. We need a book like this to refocus us and help us show our young people what the institution is supposed to be all about."

—Bookloons

"Kids will be engaged by the focus on dramatic stories, personalities, and turning points while also benefitting from the clear discussions of Congressional purpose, structure, history, and ongoing issues."

—BookTrib

ALSO AVAILABLE FROM CHICAGO REVIEW PRESS

The Industrial Revolution for Kids

The People and Technology That Changed the World, with 21 Activities

By Cheryl Mullenbach

ISBN 9781613746905

$16.95 (CAN $19.95)

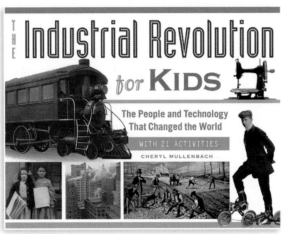

"The causes and effects of the Industrial Revolution are complex and many, and Mullenbach does a terrific job of streamlining the topic for children."

—*School Library Journal*

"Mullenbach does a wonderful job of giving the big picture, while at the same time telling the stories of lesser-known individuals who younger readers will find especially relevant. She pulls no punches, revealing the hard times as well as the good things that came out of the era."

—*Nonfiction Monday*

World War I for Kids

A History with 21 Activities

By Kent R. Rasmussen

ISBN 9781613745564

$17.95 (CAN $21.95)

"An impressive yet manageable overview of the Great War. This is a well-conceived book, and one with a trove of good artwork."

—*American History* magazine

"Every so often a really outstanding book comes along for younger readers. When a book like *World War I for Kids* comes along, it offers an opportunity that a parent should embrace."

—Bookviews by Alan Caruba

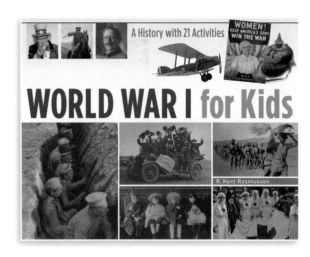

The Great Depression for Kids

Hardship and Hope in 1930s America, with 21 Activities

By Cheryl Mullenbach

ISBN 9781613730515

$16.95 (CAN $19.95)

"Mullenbach presents a thorough but readily accessible account of the Great Depression."

—*Publishers Weekly*

"The information is solid, and Mullenbach provides facts not usually found elsewhere."

—*School Library Journal*

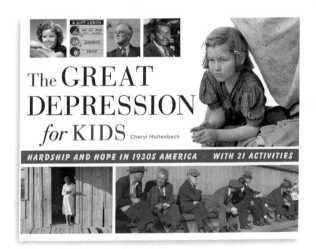

Nellie Bly and Investigative Journalism for Kids

Mighty Muckrakers from the Golden Age to Today, with 21 Activities

By Ellen Mahoney

ISBN 9781613749975

$16.95 (CAN $19.95)

"This outstanding work of nonfiction is sure to inspire a new generation of investigative journalists."

—*Teacher Librarian*

"With excellent content, an appealing layout, and an exciting topic, this book is a joy to read and explore."

—*Booklist*

CHICAGO REVIEW PRESS

Available at your favorite bookstore, by calling (800) 888-4741, or at www.chicagoreviewpress.com